MYTH OR FAITH?

Clearing Up Common Misconceptions about Christianity

STUDY GUIDE

CONCORDIA PUBLISHING HOUSE • SAINT LOUIS

Copyright © 2024 Concordia Publishing House
3558 S. Jefferson Ave., St. Louis, MO 63118-3968
1-800-325-3040 • cph.org

Written by Brian Davies, Daniel E. Paavola, Matthew Richard, Andrew R. Jones, A. Trevor Sutton, Ted Doering, Jeffrey Leininger, and Michael W. Newman

Quotations from *Luther's Works* are from Martin Luther, *Luther's Works*, American Edition; general editors: Jaroslav Pelikan, Helmut T. Lehmann, Christopher Boyd Brown, and Benjamin T. G. Mayes; 82 vols., St. Louis: Concordia Publishing House and Philadelphia: Muhlenberg and Fortress, 1955–.

Manufactured in the United States of America

1 2 3 4 5 6 7 8 9 10 33 32 31 30 29 28 27 26 25 24

Contents

SESSION 1 ABOUT GOD 5

SESSION 2 ABOUT SALVATION 25

SESSION 3 ABOUT THE BIBLE 45

SESSION 4 ABOUT BELIEF 63

SESSION 5 ABOUT THE CHURCH 81

SESSION 6 ABOUT THE SACRAMENTS 101

SESSION 7 ABOUT WORSHIP AND PRAYER 117

SESSION 8 ABOUT THE WORLD 139

ABOUT GOD

MISCONCEPTIONS ABOUT GOD

- **The doctrine of the Trinity was made up by humans.**
- **Jesus descended into hell to take the eternal punishment we deserve.**
- **The Holy Spirit is a cosmic force or universal wisdom that fills all people.**

Opening Prayer

Almighty God, praise to You and adoration for the gift of Your Word. In it, You have made Yourself known to us, and through Your Word, we know the full extent of Your love for us in Christ Jesus. Open our hearts and minds through this study of Your Word, that through it, we may know You better and be better equipped to love and serve our neighbor. Through Jesus Christ, our Lord. Amen.

Introduction

Generally speaking, the family waiting area of a major hospital is not where you want to find yourself. It's where I was one gray and overcast winter afternoon alongside a family friend who was waiting for news about his son. I was there to provide love and support for him and to join him in praying to the Lord on behalf of his son. After I had received the latest updates and checked in on how he and his wife were doing as parents, the family friend turned to spiritual things, saying, "I'm not much of a spiritual person, as you might know. But maybe you could talk to the big man upstairs about this. Not sure He wants to hear much from me, but maybe He'll listen to you. I've never needed Him more than I do right now."

While these were not easy words to hear and process, I was actually so glad he brought it up and that he was so honest with me about what he thought about God and His presence in this situation. His comments, although laden with feelings of guilt and filled with misconceptions about God, served as a nice bridge for me to talk about who God was, His care for my friend's young son, and His presence in our lives.

In this session, we are going to address some common misconceptions about God, and as you likely are aware, there are many! Unfortunately, people often view God as angry with them, aloof, disconnected from their lives, and unknowable. These misconceptions often exist for people because no one has taken the time to patiently reveal the God of the Bible to them. However, in the Scriptures, we see that God has endeavored to make Himself known to us as a God of power, wisdom, grace, mercy, and so much more. And we see this most clearly in Christ Jesus. As it is written: "For in Him the whole fullness of deity dwells bodily" (Colossians 2:9).

Because all we need to know about God has been written in the Bible for us, we'll address these common misconceptions by using the Holy Scriptures as our anchor. This chapter is not so much what I want you to know about God, or say about God, but what *the Bible* wants you to know about God and says about God! Speaking about all that is recorded in the Bible about the Lord, John writes, "But these are written so that you may believe that Jesus is the Christ, the Son of God, and that by believing you may have life in His name" (John 20:31). Said another way, we have everything we need in the Bible to help us know about God, address these misconceptions, and grow in our faith!

To help us address and process each misconception, I'll provide some Bible verses that will guide and direct our answers. Remember, all that we discover together will be rooted in the Word of God. Let's get going!

Was the doctrine of the Trinity made up by humans?

Any study or discussion about who God is must first be rooted in how God describes Himself to us. And all over the Scriptures, God reveals Himself as triune or as a Trinity, meaning one God, three persons. God is one, as we know from the Scriptures. In Deuteronomy 6:4, the Word of God says, "Hear, O Israel: The LORD our God, the LORD is one." Yet God has also revealed Himself to humanity in three distinct persons—the Father, the

Son (Jesus), and the Holy Spirit. We'll unpack what makes each person unique through some reflection questions.

So, what is the doctrine of the Trinity?

Interestingly enough, while the words *Trinity* or *triune* do not appear in the Bible, the concept of the Trinity is all over the Holy Scriptures! Like all of orthodox Christianity, The Lutheran Church—Missouri Synod adheres to the doctrine of the Trinity. The doctrine of the Trinity is a fundamental Christian belief that God exists as three distinct persons—the Father, the Son, and the Holy Spirit—while remaining one God.

God as triune is clearly expressed in the three Ecumenical Creeds of the Christian Church—the Apostles' Creed, the Nicene Creed, and the Athanasian Creed. These creeds affirm the equality and coeternality of the three persons of the Trinity. The Father, Son, and Holy Spirit are distinct persons who each share the same essence or substance. Additionally, each person of the Trinity has a unique role in the work of salvation, with the Father as the Creator, the Son as the Redeemer, and the Holy Spirit as the Sanctifier.

Rather than relying on one passage that points to God as triune, the doctrine of the Trinity is derived from the overall teaching of the entirety of the Scriptures. The concept of the Trinity is best understood by examining various passages that collectively reveal the three persons of the Godhead—the Father, the Son, and the Holy Spirit—each with distinct roles yet beautifully and in great unity sharing the same divine essence. Yet in all of this, remember that the concept of the Trinity is so grand and so divine that our attempts to explain it using mere words or to fully understand it often fall short. God is God, and we are not, and that's a good thing!

1. **Read Matthew 3:13–17. The Baptism of Jesus provides a vivid manifestation of the trinitarian nature of God. We see the Father, the Son, and the Holy Spirit all active in this moment. Where does the Trinity appear in this passage? How is each person of the Trinity active in unique ways?**

In this passage, we witness all three persons of the Trinity present and active: Jesus, the Son, being baptized; the Holy Spirit descending like a dove; and the voice of God the Father affirming and declaring His pleasure. It's a profound moment where the Father, Son, and Holy Spirit are distinctly revealed, illustrating their unity in purpose and mission.

The Baptism of Jesus serves as a powerful trinitarian revelation, highlighting the unique roles of each person within the Godhead. This event is a foundational passage for understanding the trinitarian nature of God in Christian theology.

2. **Matthew 28:18–20, often referred to as the Great Commission, is another key passage that reveals the trinitarian nature of God. What does this passage reveal about the nature of the Trinity?**

The Great Commission encapsulates the trinitarian nature of God in the Christian understanding. It emphasizes the disciples' involvement with all three persons of the Trinity—baptizing in the name of the Father, Son, and Holy Spirit—while highlighting the unified mission and divine authority of the triune God. Matthew 28:18–20 serves as a foundational biblical passage that explicitly mentions the triune God in the context of the mission and ministry of the church, emphasizing the relationship and unity among the Father, Son, and Holy Spirit.

3. **So, who are the persons of the Trinity? Numerous passages in the Old and New Testaments reveal the persons of the Trinity. What does each Bible passage below tell us about that person of the Trinity?**

- **Isaiah 64:8:**
- **Matthew 6:9 (part of the Lord's Prayer):**
- **John 1:1–14:**
- **Colossians 1:15–20:**

- **Hebrews 1:1–4:** ....

....

....

....

- **John 14:15–17:** ....

....

....

....

- **John 16:7–15:** ....

....

....

....

- **Acts 2:1–4:** ....

....

....

....

Collectively, here is what these passages reveal:

- **The Father:** Identified as the Creator, the one to be hallowed in prayer, and the sender of the Son and the Holy Spirit
- **The Son (Jesus Christ)**: Described as the Word, the exact imprint of God's nature, the image of the invisible God, and the one through whom all things were created and reconciled
- **The Holy Spirit**: Promised by Jesus as the Helper, the Spirit of truth, and the one who convicts the world concerning sin, righteousness, and judgment

These verses collectively contribute to the biblical foundation for understanding the persons of the Trinity in Christian theology. As we discussed above, all Christian doctrine is solely rooted in what has been made known to us in the Word of God. We do not base any understanding upon the teachings of church history or the revelations that come from a church leader. Rather, the Word of God alone is our guide. These passages clearly make known that God has revealed Himself as triune—Father, Son, and Holy Spirit. Although some elements and aspects may be difficult or challenging for our minds to fully grasp, it doesn't change who God is—the Holy Trinity. Based on these clear teachings of our Lord, we can say with confidence that the doctrine of the Trinity was not made up by humans, but that it is how God reveals Himself to us in His Word.

Did Jesus descend into hell to take the eternal punishment we deserve?

Having looked at the doctrine of the Trinity, we now turn our attention to a common misconception regarding hell. For a whole host of reasons, it is often thought that the descent of Jesus into hell was part of the judgment and wrath that Christ endured on our behalf, an extension, if you will, of what He endured on the cross of Calvary. But is this how we are to understand it? What does the Bible teach about Jesus' descent into hell? Let's take a look together!

1. **What is hell? To answer this question, we again must turn to the Word of God. Both the Old and New Testaments address the existence of hell, so a complete answer requires us to explore relevant biblical passages in both Testaments. What does each passage reveal about hell?**

- **Job 17:13–16:**
- **Matthew 25:46:**
- **Mark 9:43–48:**
- **Luke 16:19–31:**

- **Romans 2:5–8:**

- **2 Thessalonians 1:9:**

- **Revelation 20:10:**

Looking at all of these passages, a common thread about hell is the idea of eternal separation from God. Whether described as a place of fire, outer darkness, or torment, the central aspect is the absence of the divine presence. Additionally, fire is a recurring symbol associated with judgment. The imagery of darkness is also used to convey separation from the light of God's presence. Hell is a place of divine judgment reserved for those who stand in rejection of God.

2. If not in hell, when and how did Jesus bear our punishment?

The death of Jesus Christ serves as the ultimate expression of God's love and the only means by which humanity finds redemption. This is what we call the substitutionary atonement—the biblically revealed reality that Jesus Christ, as our substitute, bore the punishment for our sins on the cross.

3. **Substitutionary atonement, a foundational doctrine within Christian theology, asserts that Jesus Christ served as a substitute for humanity, taking upon Himself the punishment that we deserved for our sins. This concept is deeply rooted in biblical passages that depict Jesus as the sacrificial Lamb, the offering that reconciles humanity with God. What does each passage below reveal about substitutionary atonement?**

- Mark 10:45:

- 2 Corinthians 5:21:

4. **Make no mistake, this substitutionary atonement is necessary! The Bible clearly articulates what the punishment for sin is and God's solution for it. What does each passage tell us about this?**

- **Genesis 3:6–7:**
- **Romans 6:23:**
- **Leviticus 16:11–17:**
- **Genesis 3:15:**

The New Testament, then, presents Jesus as the fulfillment of these messianic promises. John the Baptist identifies Him as the Lamb of God, who takes away the sin of the world (John 1:29). The Gospels narrate His life, teachings, and the ultimate sacrifice on the cross as the culmination of God's redemptive plan.

The Bible speaks of God's righteous wrath against sin. Romans 1:18 asserts that the wrath of God is revealed against all ungodliness and unrighteousness. This wrath is not arbitrary anger but a just response to the violation of God's moral order—our sin against God and neighbor.

Jesus Christ is then sent by God as mediator. The role of Jesus as the mediator between God and humanity is emphasized in 1 Timothy 2:5. As the perfect mediator, Jesus reconciles us to God by bearing the punishment that our sins deserved.

Understanding the depth of Jesus' substitutionary atonement leads to profound gratitude. Christians are called to respond with lives of worship, recognizing the sacrificial love that redeemed them. The awareness of Christ's substitutionary sacrifice motivates believers to pursue holiness. Romans 12:1 calls for presenting our bodies as living sacrifices, responding to the mercy received through Christ. Additionally, the commission given by Jesus in Matthew 28:18–20 calls believers to share the Good News of salvation, emphasizing the role of Jesus as the substitute who reconciles humanity with God.

The death of Jesus Christ, viewed through the lens of substitutionary atonement, stands as the pinnacle of God's redemptive plan for humanity. Second Corinthians 5:21 serves as a poignant, clarifying truth of the profound exchange that occurred on the cross, where Jesus bore the punishment for our sins, offering us His righteousness. The theological implications of sin separating us from God, our need for a Savior, and the wrath of God find resolution in the person and work of Jesus Christ. In the grand narrative of the Bible, the death of Jesus emerges as the ultimate act of divine love, reconciling a broken relationship and providing hope for all who believe.

This is all accomplished on the cross, not through the cross coupled with a descent into hell.

So, if not to bear our punishment, then why *did* Jesus descend into hell?

The Apostles' Creed, the oldest and most widely accepted creed in the Christian Church, includes the statement "He descended into hell." The same language is used in the Athanasian Creed. The phrase has been a source of some confusion, and it's worth taking some time to unpack how we understand it.

Christian theologians often distinguish between "the state of humiliation" and "the state of exultation" in understanding the person and work of Jesus. The state of humiliation encompasses His incarnation, suffering, and death, while the state of exultation involves His resurrection, ascension, and glorification.

The crucifixion stands as the epitome of Jesus' state of humiliation. The physical and spiritual agony experienced on the cross reflect the taking of the full weight of our sin upon Himself, as we discussed above.

Contrary to being a continuation of His state of humiliation, the descent into hell is seen as an aspect of Jesus' state of exultation. Rather than a continuation of His suffering, it is a proclamation of victory over sin, death, and the powers of darkness.

5. **Read 1 Peter 3:18–19. What does this crucial text tell us about Jesus' descent into hell? How does it show the descent as part of Jesus' state of exultation?**

The descent of Jesus into hell, as professed in the Apostles' and Athanasian Creeds, is a complex element of Christian doctrine. No wonder people have misconceptions! Contrary to being a continuation of His state of humiliation, it is a proclamation of victory over sin, death, and the forces of darkness. The theological significance lies in the assurance that, in Christ, believers share in His triumph and have hope in the face of death. The descent into hell, as part of Jesus' state of exultation, reaffirms the centrality of His redemptive work and the ultimate victory achieved on behalf of humanity. As Christians reflect on this profound aspect of their faith, it invites contemplation on the richness of Christ's work and the hope that it imparts to those who believe and trust in Him.

Is the Holy Spirit a cosmic force or universal wisdom that fills all people?

What an interestingly phrased question, right? The wording itself reveals the extent of the confusion regarding the Holy Spirit. There are many factors and causes that lead to this confusion. Of all the persons of the Trinity, the Holy Spirit, more than the others, lacks a human comparable.

Follow me here. We have a bit of a handle on God the Father because we know what fathers are like. We have them, and we see them in the world and in our culture. And we have a bit of a handle on Jesus because He lived for a period as a Jewish carpenter and traveling preacher and miracle-worker in first-century Palestine. The Holy Spirit, on the other hand, is . . . a spirit. How exactly do you describe or get a handle on or understand a spirit? In this section, we'll explore what we know about the Holy Spirit, the work that He does, and how we can be sure He dwells within us. And as is our practice, we'll use the Word of God as our anchor and source. Let's go!

1. **Who is the Holy Spirit? While some mistakenly think the Holy Spirit didn't arrive in the Bible until the Pentecost event in Acts 2, the reality is that the Holy Spirit has always been active. In the Old Testament, the Holy Spirit is referred to using various Hebrew terms. The word *Ruach* denotes the Spirit of God, emphasizing His presence, power, and breath. In the New Testament, He plays a crucial role in the incarnation of Christ and His church. What insights does each passage below reveal about the person, role, and transformative work of the Holy Spirit?**

- **Genesis 1:2:**
- **Genesis 1:26–27:**

- **Judges 6:34:**

- **Luke 1:35:**

- **Matthew 3:16–17:**

- **Matthew 12:28:**

- **John 14:16–17:**

- **John 3:5–8:**

- **1 Corinthians 6:19:**

- **Acts 2:**

- **Romans 8:26–27:**

- **Acts 15:28:**

- **Acts 8:29:**

- **Ephesians 4:30:**

The Holy Spirit, as revealed in the Bible, emerges as a dynamic and personal entity within the Godhead, with a mind, will, and agency. From the Old Testament's creative and empowering presence to the New Testament's revelation of His redemptive work, the Holy Spirit plays a multifaceted role in the unfolding drama of salvation. The biblical narrative paints a rich tapestry of the Holy Spirit's personhood, part of the triune God, drawing people to the Lord, keeping them in faith, and empowering them to bring light and life in Jesus to an unbelieving world.

2. **The Bible unfolds a profound narrative of the divine workings of the Holy Spirit in the world. In the previous question, we addressed who the Holy Spirit *is*. Now let's look at what He *does*. While it's difficult to separate the identity of the Holy Spirit from His work and actions, as He is best understood by what He does, let's drill down into the Bible texts that focus on His works. What does each passage tell us about what the Holy Spirit *does*?**

- **John 15:26–27:**

- **John 16:7–8:**

- **John 16:12–14:**

- **1 Corinthians 12:4–11:**

- **Galatians 5:22–23:**

- **Romans 8:11:**

- **Romans 8:26–27:**

God, through the Holy Spirit, is busy! From testifying to the truth and convicting the world of sin to guiding believers into all truth, distributing diverse spiritual gifts, producing fruits of the Spirit, activating resurrection power, and interceding in weakness, the Holy Spirit's multifaceted presence is evident.

Having unpacked biblically the person and work of the Holy Spirit, we now turn our attention to how we can be sure that this gift lives in us. How can I know whether I have the Holy Spirit? To answer this question, we'll explore together the biblical foundation for the certainty of having the Holy Spirit, emphasizing the role of Baptism as the moment when believers receive this precious gift.

3. **What do the following passages tell us about how the Holy Spirit is given to believers through the Sacrament of Holy Baptism, providing a profound and lasting assurance that the Lord truly dwells in us?**

- **Acts 2:38:**
- **Matthew 3:13–17:**
- **Ephesians 1:13–14:**

- **Titus 3:5–7:**

- **Acts 10:44–48:**

- **Colossians 2:11–12:**

Christians can be certain that in their Baptism, they have received the Holy Spirit. This is the Lord's promise to them. From the promise of the Spirit in Acts 2:38 to the baptismal formula in Matthew 28:19, and from the seal of the Holy Spirit in Ephesians 1:13–14 to the clarity of Titus 3:5–7, the Bible consistently underscores the transformative and assuring role of Baptism in securing the Holy Spirit's presence in the lives of believers. The Sacrament of Baptism, grounded in faith and obedience to Christ's command, serves as the moment when the Holy Spirit is received, marking the beginning of a profound and enduring relationship between God and His people. As believers, the assurance of the Holy Spirit becomes a source of comfort, guidance, and empowerment, shaping their identity as children of God and empowering them to live out their faith in the world.

So, would we call the Holy Spirit a "cosmic force"? No, because that implies His origins are unknown and His gifts and benefits unknowable. Would we call Him a "universal wisdom that fills all people"? Again, no, because He's way more than wisdom, and the Spirit is not given haphazardly. Instead, we understand the Holy Spirit as a person of the triune God; that in addition to the many gifts He brings, He chiefly points us to Jesus Christ; and that we can be certain that this Holy Spirit dwells in us because we have received the gift of Holy Baptism. Thanks be to God!

Closing Prayer

> *Almighty God, Father, Son, and Holy Spirit, praise to You and adoration for how You have made Yourself known to us and to all of humanity. Continue to lead us, we pray, to a richer understanding of Your Word, that we might love You with our whole hearts and love and serve our neighbors. May Your kingdom come and Your will be done. We ask this in Jesus' name. Amen.*

ABOUT SALVATION

MISCONCEPTIONS ABOUT SALVATION

- **Jesus is our helper and guide through life, an example to demonstrate what the Christian life is like.**
- **There is a limit to God's forgiveness.**
- **Christians need to be afraid of Judgment Day.**

Opening Prayer

Heavenly Father, You sent Your Son to live among us, fulfilling all the Law demanded and then, by His death, paying the penalty for our sins. Keep us in the faith You've given us through the Spirit. Draw us each day closer to You in understanding Your Word and in service to You. We pray in Jesus' name. Amen.

Introduction

Perhaps the most essential question we could ask is "How can I be saved eternally?" All of our other worries retreat in the presence of this crucial question. However, asking what I must do to be saved starts the question in the wrong direction. The joyful truth is that we are saved by God's mercy and grace, received by the faith that He gives us. Perhaps we should ask, "How has God saved me through the work of His Son?" That is the heart of our salvation.

Is Jesus just a good example for us, a helper or guide to demonstrate the Christian life?

When we were little, we wanted to do it ourselves. We insisted that we could tie our own shoes, choose our own clothes, and decide what we wanted to eat. Remember how we wanted to leave our shoes untied, wear only the same red shirt, and never eat broccoli? While all those choices will change in time, the wise parent knows that a child needs direction and often help. So, when we view Jesus, we might see Him as the heavenly source of direction and occasional help. We imagine that saving ourselves is something we can do if we have just a bit of help from Jesus. But Jesus came to save us entirely by His life, death, and resurrection. This is a gift of eternal life. It's not an impossible burden or an example beyond following.

1. **What is the best gift you've ever received? How much did you see it coming? Now think of all the gifts God gives us. What was His most essential gift?**

2. **What was Jesus' essential reason for coming? How did He accomplish that purpose? Read John 3:13–17. (For further background concerning Moses and the bronze serpent, you can also go to Numbers 21:4–9.)**

Jesus came not as a condemning judge but as the single Savior of the world. This passage shows how God cures through the illness itself. The cure for the poisonous snake bite was to look at the bronze serpent. So, Jesus placed Himself on the cross, condemned by many and bearing the sins of the world. But it is the Savior on the cross that gives us hope. What love He has brought even through His death!

3. **How can looking at Jesus on the cross give us hope and comfort? How does viewing the cross draw us together in our worship and our sharing of the Gospel message?**

By the work of the Spirit, we are drawn to Jesus, hearing God's message of forgiveness in this striking moment of the death of His Son. At the death of His Son, God returns the light to the world (see Matthew 27:45 and Luke 23:44). Upon the death of Jesus, God finishes the work of saving the world. See Colossians 1:20, where God makes peace with the world through the blood of His cross. We might hear God declare, "You have killed My Son. Peace be to you!" What an astonishing turn that fulfills the purpose of His coming—to save the world.

Therefore, God chooses to see us through the lens of the life of Jesus. By doing that, God can both save us and also satisfy the demands of justice.

4. **Read Romans 3:23–26. What wonderful parallel does Paul makes here?**

So, Jesus poured His perfect life into our account so that God could count us as righteous entirely by what Jesus has done. When our conscience accuses us of our failures, we can acknowledge that we are far from perfect. We can also admit that our future will fail also. But Christ did not come to condemn us and leave us broken. God doesn't deal with us according to our failure but according to the purpose of Jesus' coming. He came that we might be the washed, saved, and renewed people of God, standing on His perfect life and death.

5. **As you were growing up, what were your favorite ways of helping your parents or older siblings?**

As children, we wanted to be a part of the family's work and projects. While we might not have been a great help in washing the car, mixing the cake batter, or making our bed, we wanted to be a grown-up helper and partner. Our parents gave us jobs that we could safely do, while they did the actual work.

6. **Since Jesus came to save the world, is there anything that we need to do in the work of our salvation? Or are we simply swept up by God's mercy and deposited in heaven? Read Acts 16:25–34, which describes the night Paul and Silas were in the jail in Philippi, as you consider these questions.**

7. **In such a crisis moment, how is Paul's answer enough to turn the jailer from despair to hope? Once the jailer has heard Paul's answer, what questions might he have for Paul concerning Jesus and the life He offers?**

8. **John gives a clear summary of Jesus and our faith at the end of his Gospel. Read John 20:30–31. What three essential actions do we see in this passage?**

We must first know that Jesus is the Son of God, the Savior of the world, and this we know by reading the Word, especially the four Gospels. We are given this knowledge by the power of the Holy Spirit working through the words of Jesus' life.

Besides knowing the identity of Jesus as the Christ, the anointed Savior of the world, we must also believe in Him. It is one thing to know the witness of the Gospel message that Jesus is the Savior. It is another step to believe that He is the Savior of the whole world and therefore the Savior of ourselves. Knowledge of the Gospel witness is wonderful, but simply knowing the biblical record is not enough. Faith, which is a gift from the Holy Spirit, trusts that Jesus is my Savior. We can have this confidence from Bible verses that speak of God's work for all people. We might doubt that God would wish to save us, but we cannot deny that we are human and therefore part of the whole world that God has forgiven through Christ.

9. **Read 2 Corinthians 5:19, which illustrates the previous point. How could God not put the blame for our wrongs on us? If the guilt is not on us, where does it go?**

Finally, by knowing Jesus and believing in Him, we have life through Him. In John 10:10, Jesus says, "I came that they may have life and have it abundantly." In that abundant life, we know that God is with us, that we are forgiven our sins, and that we have the indwelling power of the Holy Spirit each day. We not only have God's presence now, but we also have the promise of eternal life. This is the abundant life Jesus gives now and forever.

10. **Jesus is the perfect Son of God. We hear God the Father say at Jesus' Baptism, "You are My beloved Son; with You I am well pleased" (Luke 3:22). In the book of Hebrews, Jesus is described as the perfect High Priest who needs no sacrifice for Himself since He is perfect. Read Hebrews 7:23–26 and discuss the contrasts between imperfect human priests and Jesus as the ultimate, perfect priest.**

11. **Since Jesus is perfect, how can we, imperfect as we are, be anywhere near Him? Read Hebrews 5:9. What was the purpose of His perfection?**

12. **Failure tends to drive us away from those who are perfect. Not so with Jesus. How does the perfection of Jesus attract us to Him even when we are so far from perfection ourselves? Read Hebrews 4:15–16 as you reflect.**

Jesus is the ideal person and life—the only one to complete every commandment every day. But that perfection is not a selfish achievement for Himself. His record is given to us so that we are seen by God as perfect. God, the righteous judge, declares us to be innocent even though we are thoroughly guilty. But He can make that judgment by the perfection of Jesus given to us. By that mercy, we follow His lead each day. We will never match His perfection, but His perfection draws us to Himself to live thankfully each day in His mercy.

Does God's forgiveness have limits?

Everything has a price, and every family has only so much money. That mansion you drive by each day looks wonderful, but when you check the online real estate site, you find that the asking price is twice what you expected. Even things we desperately want might be out of reach. So, when we consider forgiveness of our sins, what price might be attached to that forgiveness? Besides the cost of forgiveness in this moment, consider that our debt with God only increases every day. Are we completely outside the price of God's forgiveness? That is a great concern, but the wonderful news is that God's forgiveness is limitless. It comes at the great cost of His Son's death, but the benefit of that death comes to us without a price. He covers the sins of the world. Therefore, He forgives each of us.

1. **In the face of our sin, sometimes forgiveness can seem impossible. How can God forgive me when I've done so many bad things? But let's approach this from a different direction. How many times have you had to redo a project or attempted to solve a problem? When has it happened that you found you were going in the wrong direction—tightening the pickle jar lid instead of opening it?**

The forgiveness of our sins is the crucial project we face. If shooting free throws or understanding calculus requires some help, then all the more, the forgiveness of sins cannot be done by our strength alone. Forgiveness comes only when we realize that we cannot pay for our past or perfect our future. The Holy Spirit leads us to see the truth of our sins, not in comparison to someone else, but simply as our unchanged evil. Then we are ready to hear the mercy of God and receive His forgiveness by faith. This won't be our work, but rather the work of God through the promises of the Gospel.

2. **Read Luke 18:9–14 to see the contrast of the two men both seeking the approval of God. How did the Pharisee attempt to gain the favor of God? What do people today put on their list of accomplishments to attempt to gain favor with God?**

3. **Now consider the tax collector. Why was his short prayer heard (Luke 18:13–14)? Why did it bring forgiveness to the man?**

Another man much like the tax collector, fully aware of his failures, was the apostle Paul. Paul had been a Pharisee who tried to achieve righteousness through his keeping of the Law (see Philippians 3:4–6). However, when Jesus stopped Paul on the road to Damascus and turned his life around, Paul realized that he was the worst sinner.

4. **Read 1 Timothy 1:12–16 to see how Paul viewed his past but then also how God showed His grace through the failures of Paul. How could Paul see himself as the worst sinner and yet also as an example for the world?**

Paul said that he was the worst sinner in the world. At our lowest moments, we feel we could argue with Paul about that. But the point is not finding the longest list of sins, but rather knowing that no matter what we have done, we have been redeemed by the perfect patience and mercy of God in Christ. Our failures are many, and listing them would be endless. But the sacrifice of Jesus' perfect life in our place brings forgiveness as God sees the value of His Son's life as equal to the cost of every sin. While we cannot pay for even one soul, the priceless life and death of God's Son was worth the world to His Father. It is not our value that gives us peace, but the holy and precious life and blood of Jesus that is our security.

First Peter 1:18–19 tells us about the power and value of the "precious blood of Jesus" in redeeming us all. Jesus offered Himself, losing His life on the cross, that He might pay the ransom for the entire world. Therefore, though our sins are many, His mercy is greater, and the worth of His life, death, and resurrection pay every debt for each of us.

5. **When have you suddenly gotten what you never expected: the perfect parking spot is open, the grocery checkout line has no one in it, or they posted a 25 percent sale on what you were going to buy anyway?**

The offer of forgiveness is the ultimate gift, but a gift that leaves us asking, "How has God made forgiveness possible for us?" It's wonderful news, this promise of free, full forgiveness of all our sins for all time. But how has God done this for us, and especially for me? I can imagine the very best people in the world getting this offer, but not me.

We can understand how God brings forgiveness to us with these two phrases: by grace, through faith. By understanding those few words, we can understand how God can bring forgiveness to the world, and we are drawn to that forgiveness as a genuine promise of God intended for each of us.

6. **We begin with the gift of grace, which is the unexpected and undeserved mercy of God. It is the motivation of God to forgive the world. Read Ephesians 2:1–9 for a wonderful expression of grace at work in bringing us God's justification. According to this passage, how can God view us, by grace, as beloved and justified, even though we've done nothing to deserve this love and mercy?**

7. **Read Romans 3:21–26. How does this comfort us and speak to our doubts about whether our sins are too much for God to forgive?**

8. **When have you been given a gift that leaves you asking, "Really? This is for me?"**

The gift of forgiveness by grace leaves us asking if this could actually be true. God's forgiveness of all we have done plus the gift of eternal life with Him is beyond any victory, lottery win, or promotion we might receive. Since we know it is a gift of grace beyond anything we have received, we have to ask how this can be. That's when our second phrase comes to the front. We are saved through faith. Through faith alone, we receive the forgiveness that we can never earn or deserve. A true gift doesn't require a repayment plan. In fact, offering to repay the cost of the gift misses the whole point of a gift. A gift is received through faith by the mercy and generosity of the giver.

So, we receive the gift of mercy through faith. Romans 4:16 offers a clear picture of this sequence of a gift received through faith since it came by grace. See also Galatians 2:16, where Paul explains that the gift of being just in God's eyes is received through faith, not by any of our actions.

9. **What was the easiest job you ever had that you still got paid for?**

10. **Read Romans 4:3–5. What is distinctive about the nature of the faith of Abraham?**

No one would walk up to a pay window and ask for a paycheck if they had done nothing and had not even been on the jobsite. But the offer of God's mercy draws us forward to receive God's forgiveness when we have done nothing. Faith alone trusts the promise that the treasure of forgiveness is real and intended for us. The Spirit works through the word of these promises and gives us the gift of faith so that, in thanks, we trust His offer of forgiveness and receive it through faith alone. By grace, received through faith, God makes forgiveness possible for each of us.

11. **Do we need to change our lives before God will forgive us? To help us think about this question, consider times when you might say, "I have to change my clothes before we go." On the other hand, where can you go just as you are, any time, any day?**

Do we need to change, to dress up for God before He will see us? On the one hand, that makes perfect sense. If you were to have a once-in-a-lifetime audience with God, wouldn't you wear your absolute best? In fact, forget what's in your closet now. Rent, buy, or borrow something much better.

But is that God's demand? No, He is the complete opposite, as He welcomes sinners in every state.

12. Read Luke 15:11–32, the parable of the prodigal son. How did the son appear when he returned home? How much did it matter to his father that he was penniless and hungry? How is the son a picture of our own meeting with God?

13. Let's look at another image of God taking someone just as he was. Read Luke 19:1–10. Unlike the prodigal son, Zacchaeus was rich but was hidden in a tree as Jesus walked past him. Jesus called him down and invited Himself to Zacchaeus's house for a meal. Why was Zacchaeus overjoyed to welcome Jesus to his house? Why would Jesus' enemies object to Him dining with Zacchaeus?

14. A final dramatic illustration of Jesus' welcome and protection for someone who was in deep trouble is the woman caught in adultery. Read John 8:1–11 for her story. Jesus causes all her accusers to leave since none of them are without sin. What wonderful question does Jesus ask her in verse 10? How might she have felt as she answered Jesus? What balance of mercy and new direction does Jesus give her in verse 11?

In summary, God accepts people in their worst moments without hesitation. Sinners don't need to become something they will never be—perfectly holy. But God has forgiven us already through the death and resurrection of Jesus. Being forgiven by grace alone, we are glad to follow Jesus in a renewed life. The changes that we experience are all because He has already loved and forgiven us. We walk in a renewed life as witness to His mercy alone.

At first, it makes sense that we have to do something to come near to God. It seems we should be perfect if we hope to have His blessing. But the grace of God welcomes us as we are, coming in humility, confessing our sins. There is no limit to His grace. God has already forgiven us and all the world through Christ, so we come to receive that forgiveness through faith alone. Having been forgiven, we live new lives in appreciation of all God has done by His grace alone.

Should Christians be afraid of Judgment Day?

Judgment Day has an ominous sound. We likely have images of a bolt of lightning splitting open the heavens and then a frightening interrogation at the gates of eternity. The line is long, not moving, and we are at the very end. But we have little to no hope anyway. If there is a recounting of our lives, we are doomed.

However, contrary to those images, the Scriptures give us a different picture. Jesus returns as the Shepherd to gather His sheep. He comes as the God who has already forgiven the world through His own sacrifice. His coming again is not a frightening day of doom but the day the church has eagerly awaited. He comes to raise the dead, gather His own to eternal life, and never let them go. We can say with the church for all time, "Amen. Come, Lord Jesus!" (Revelation 22:20).

Judgment Day could be the ultimate worst day on the calendar. If we picture Judgment Day as a thorough exam of our every day, every act, and every word, then we naturally live in dread of it coming. And its coming is even worse than a chemistry test. At least you knew when the chemistry test was happening. But Judgment Day might come any day, any moment. Viewing Judgment Day that way, we would live under a constant cloud of doom.

However, that is not how God describes the return of Jesus and the gift of resurrection and the entrance into heaven for all who believe in Jesus as the Savior. We who live in faith in Jesus know that He will come to bring the resurrection of the dead and the entrance to heaven. With that faith, His coming is the best day we can imagine.

So, what does the Bible say about Judgment Day?

1. **Read 1 Thessalonians 4:13–18 as Paul describes the return of Jesus and the resurrection of the dead. Based on this passage, where today are the souls of those who have died in faith in Jesus? When Jesus returns, what will happen to these souls of those who have died and their bodies?**

Let's look at another image of Judgment Day—one that is often misunderstood. To understand this image correctly, we need to remember that we are saved by God's grace alone and not our work.

2. **Read Matthew 25:31–46, where Jesus describes dividing of the world as sheep and goats when He returns. In this passage, how does it appear that one is saved or lost? How is this view different from the 1 Thessalonians 4:13–18 reading?**

If we were to read Matthew 25:31–46 alone, we might conclude that we are saved on Judgment Day by the charity and kindness we have shown in our lives. However, that view contradicts the truth that we are saved by grace alone, not by any of our works. See Ephesians 2:8–9 for this truth. The good that believers do is seen as good by God because of God's grace. Note that in the Matthew 25 text, the believers are saved without any comparison between those who are saved. God's justification of us through Christ's work comes first so that any kindness we do is a result of being saved, not the cause of our salvation.

The kindness to others noted in Matthew 25 can be a witness to God's greater mercy, which saves us. Notice that those who are saved are not expecting to be saved by what they have done. They are gathered as the sheep, the flock God has saved, by His choice and action.

Therefore, we can look ahead to Jesus' return and Judgment Day as a time when God's gracious promises will be fulfilled. He comes to lift our bodies from death to life and to gather us as His eternal flock, the people for whom He has prepared heaven.

3. **Just as Christians do not need to fear Judgment Day, neither do we need to fear death. What hope do Christians have in the face of death?**

When Christians face death, the Spirit brings us words that give hope. More than empty promises or fragile hopes, these are the strong promises of God. Let's consider some of them now.

4. **Read Romans 6:1–11. What has Baptism done for our union with Jesus and His death and resurrection? How can Paul be certain that we will share Jesus' resurrection since we have already shared His death? Finally, how is Jesus' freedom from death good news for us?**

5. **Read 2 Timothy 4:6–8, where Paul speaks of his coming death and the reward that follows. How does Paul describe his life and, given his endurance, what celebration is waiting for him upon death? How does Paul describe God's gifts that will come to him and to all believers?**

Because of this coming gift of eternal life and the crown of righteousness, Paul endures the challenges of his life. Paul had no lack of hardship, imprisonment, and danger. But those things were nothing compared to what comes upon death.

6. **Read 2 Corinthians 4:17 and see the contrast that Paul describes. Troubles can multiply, but they are all nothing compared to the glory to come. See also Philippians 3:7–11, where Paul is ready to lose all things so that he might gain the resurrection. How difficult was Paul's life with his travels, imprisonments, beatings, and uncertainties? What wonders and blessings are waiting in heaven that make all those difficulties nothing in comparison?**

What joy can the Christian have in the face of death? We can stand in awe that Jesus would choose to take on the death of the cross in order to save us. He had no need to die, and no one compelled Him to die—as it says in John 10:17–18, where Jesus makes it clear that His life is laid down and taken up again all by His choice. Because He has died and risen again, we who believe in Him will also die and then be raised. Death is not the end of life, but it is the doorway to the boundless blessings of heaven. God gives us life after death, all by His mercy, so that we don't fear being condemned for our failure. We are saved by God's promises and our union with Jesus through faith in His promises of life.

7. **Where can I turn for comfort and assurance if I'm afraid of God's judgment?**

Facing both death and the judgment of God, we can't stand on our own success. We can turn to the promises of God to save His own people, and we can also see those who have heard and believed those words that bring eternal life.

8. **Perhaps the clearest example of one in need who hears the perfect word of life is in Luke 23:39–43. Read this passage about the thief on the cross and the promise of heaven. How is the setting of the cross and darkness a far cry from any vision of paradise? How does the thief show extraordinary faith? How does Jesus express wonderful power and grace in His reply?**

What astonishing faith in the midst of a cruel death. We can have that same faith that Jesus is the King who died in our place and who will return in power and mercy.

This faith in the return of Jesus leads us to another passage of great comfort.

9. **Read John 14:1–6, 18. Jesus promises both that He is preparing a place for us in heaven and also that He is going to return to gather us to be with Him. How are these promises necessary as we face death? Since He is already risen from the dead, what certainty and peace can we have of Him fulfilling these promises?**

What a joy that He who worked as a carpenter for decades now prepares a home for us in heaven. The certainty of that promise rests on the simple wood of the cross and His willingness to pay there for our entry into His kingdom. He took the lowest place so that He might bring us to the highest heights. He endured the cross for six hours so that we might spend eternity with Him.

10. **Read Romans 8:34–39 for our final reassurance of God's strong plan. Paul lists many of the enemies that threaten us. Are there one or two others that you might add to that list? Yet how has God overcome all these by His death and resurrection, and also the fact that He speaks for us?**

Perhaps we might sum up our hope with the words of Romans 8:31: "If God is for us, who can be against us?" No enemy, no threat from past or an unknown future can tear us from His love and power. No one can silence the words of Jesus on our behalf. No debt can outdo the full payment for all our sins. The hope that God gives endures through this life into the eternal life He has promised.

The judgment of God has already been announced, and it has brought God's forgiveness and peace. We have been declared righteous in God's sight by the forgiveness won on the cross. That judgment of peace between ourselves and God cannot change since it is God's own strong word. Therefore, we need not fear judgment since He has already given us His peace.

Closing Prayer

> *Our heavenly Father, thank You for the saving life, death, and resurrection of Jesus, by which You have given us the promise of heaven. Keep us in the faith in Your promises and the peace that guards our hearts. Let us not fear the end but eagerly wait for Your return. You have promised to come soon, and we can only say, "Amen. Come quickly, Lord Jesus."*

SESSION 3

ABOUT THE BIBLE

MISCONCEPTIONS ABOUT THE BIBLE

- **The New Testament is more important today than the Old Testament.**
- **You can make the Bible prove anything; it's all a matter of interpretation.**
- **There are a lot of mistakes in the Bible.**

Opening Prayer

O Lord, make me captive to Your Holy Word. May Your Bible shape, guide, and grant me assurance as I journey through life's valley of tears. Sustain me in Your eternal truth until You finally take me unto Yourself in glory. Amen.

Introduction

It has been said before that the Bible is the best-selling book of all time. A quick search on the internet will confirm this, showing that the Bible has sold over five billion copies. Now, one would think that with such a best-selling book, there would be unanimous support for the Bible, as well as a great deal of common understanding. However, if you have ever watched a documentary on the Bible on television, had a conversation with a religious-minded coffee barista at a local coffee shop, or talked to an agnostic relative at Thanksgiving, you will find very quickly that there are a plethora of questions surrounding this best-selling book.

As Christians, it is important not to avoid questions about the Bible, though, especially the hard ones. While it may seem counterintuitive, it best serves us to address the difficult questions head-on. In other words, it is wise to approach questions about the Bible with boldness. Indeed, we can boldly examine difficult questions to learn how to give a humble answer and defend the Bible from those who challenge it.

While people have many misconceptions about the Bible, we'll address three major ones, asking questions and letting Scripture guide our answers. Let us boldly and confidently examine them to be further equipped and strengthened in God's Holy Word.

Is the New Testament more important today than the Old Testament?

New is better, right? Everyone knows the most recent cell phone is better than the previous version. A newer car is better than an older car. Old things are for a previous generation; new things are for the here and now, right? To a certain extent, this is correct. However, is this true with the Bible? Is the New Testament better than the Old Testament, as if the New Testament is running 2.0 software and the Old Testament is running 1.0? Let's walk through these questions together.

1. **Is the Old Testament only Law? One of the disparaging comments about the Old Testament is that it supposedly contains irrelevant laws about shellfish (see Leviticus 11:12) and haircuts (see Leviticus 19:27). Have you heard comments like these? Take a moment to read those verses. Do they sound strange to you?**

While many laws in the Old Testament may seem peculiar to the modern reader, just because something seems peculiar to our modern ear does not mean that it is automatically irrelevant. For example, in Leviticus 19:27, the Israelites were told not to "round off the hair on [their] temples or mar the edges of [their] beard." The reason? Because that is how certain cults of the dead cut their hair and trimmed their beards. This seemingly peculiar and obscure law about not cutting hair makes sense when understood within a particular context.

Why would the Israelites, who belonged to the life-giving God, cut their hair to resemble those in cults of death?

Sometimes—maybe because of the movies—people reduce the Old and New Testaments to a man and a mountain: Moses receiving the Ten Commandments on Mount Sinai (Law) and Jesus on Mount Calvary (Gospel). While this observation may have validity, it is important to remember that Moses spoke both words of Law and words of Gospel. And Jesus? He, too, spoke words of Law and words of Gospel.

2. **Read the following passages. Which ones are words of Law? Which ones are words of Gospel?**

- **Isaiah 1:18:**
- **Mark 10:19:**
- **Psalm 103:12:**
- **Isaiah 43:1:**
- **Genesis 3:15:**
- **Matthew 5:21–48:**

So, both the Old and New Testaments contain Law—what we should and should not do—and both the Old and New Testaments contain the Gospel—what God has promised and done for humanity.

3. **Is the Old Testament about Israel and not us? What's so special about Israel and the Hebrew people? Why did God call a slave nation out of Egypt to be His people? It all has to do with Genesis 12:1–3. Take a moment and read that passage. What does God promise at the end of verse 3?**

4. **But who is Abraham? Look at the following passages and discuss what they tell us about Abraham's descendants and who receives the blessing.**

- **Genesis 26:4; 28:14:**
- **Exodus 2:24:**

- **2 Samuel 7:11–16:**

5. **What exactly is this blessing? Look up the following passages and discuss what they reveal about the blessing.**

- **Isaiah 9:6–7:**

- **Isaiah 52:13–53:12:**

So what's so special about Israel? They were the nation chosen to bring forth the Messiah—the Savior—for all people! Is the Old Testament about Israel? Absolutely! Is the Old Testament about you? Absolutely! The Old Testament is the history of your salvation. It is how God worked through Israel to bring forth the Messiah for the redemption of the entire world, which includes you!

6. **Now read Galatians 3:16–18, 27–29. Do you find it comforting to hear that you are heirs according to the promise given to Abraham?**

7. **What about Jesus in the Old Testament? Read Genesis 3:15. How does this passage point to the promised Messiah?**

8. **Genesis 3:15 says there will be "enmity"—that is, hatred and hostility—between Satan and the messianic lineage of Eve. Read 1 Samuel 17:8–10, 32, 41–51 with the Genesis passage in mind. How does this familiar story also show the greater war between the offspring of Eve and the offspring of Satan?**

Is the Old Testament about Jesus? Yes, it is. You just need to follow the promise. Indeed, follow the thin red line of Jesus through the Old Testament, as evil continually works to snuff out the promise of salvation.

How did the writers of the New Testament view the Old Testament? Let's explore by looking at some parallels between the book of Matthew and the story of the exodus, of Moses leading the Hebrews out of Egypt.

The Hebrews went out from the land of Egypt (see Exodus 12:40–41).	In Matthew 2:19–23, Joseph, Mary, and Jesus left Egypt.
The Hebrews went through the Red Sea waters (see Exodus 14:21–22).	In Matthew 3:13–17, Jesus was baptized not in the Red Sea but in the Jordan River.
Following the journey through the sea, the Israelites were in the wilderness for forty years before entering the Promised Land (see Numbers 14:32–33; Joshua 1:13).	In Matthew 4:1–11, after His Baptism, Jesus went into the wilderness not for forty years but for forty days.
And finally, the Hebrews had twelve tribes (see Joshua 13–19).	After the wilderness, starting in Matthew 4:18–22, Jesus chose not twelve tribes but twelve disciples.

9. **What do the structure and events of the book of Matthew tell us about how the New Testament views the Old Testament?**

So, the New Testament sees the Old Testament not only leading and pointing to Jesus but fulfilled in Him.

10. **How did Jesus understand the Old Testament? Let's let Scripture and some of Jesus' own words instruct us. Read the following passages to hear what Jesus said about the Old Testament.**

- **Luke 24:27, 44–47:**
- **John 1:45:**
- **John 5:39, 46:**

In a word, Jesus interpreted the Old Testament according to Himself—everything in the Old Testament had to be fulfilled by Him.

11. **Are parts of the Old Testament no longer relevant? Read Acts 17:1–9, where Paul preaches and reasons with Jews in the synagogue to tell them about Jesus. What did he use to make his points? Why is that important?**

The Old Testament preaches Christ, and Christ is always relevant!

Considering this, though, are there parts of the Old Testament that are no longer applicable? To a certain extent, yes. For example, many laws in the Old Testament applied to Israel as a nation in that time period. Consider Exodus 22:1: "If a man steals an ox or a sheep, and kills it or sells it, he shall repay five oxen for an ox, and four sheep for a sheep." Embedded in this verse is the Seventh Commandment (which still applies to us today); however, the specific restitution for stealing is only applied to the people of Israel. The Old Testament also contains many laws about the sacrificial system—Leviticus 1–7, for example. These verses foreshadow Jesus' sacrifice. That is to say, all of these verses about the sacrificial system find their fulfillment in the ultimate sacrifice of Christ Jesus on the cross.

12. **The writers of the New Testament did not abandon the Old Testament as if it were irrelevant or not part of the Christian faith. In fact, they deliberately connected their work to the Old Testament by using its quotations, allusions, and concepts (hundreds of times, if not more). How does this help us understand the Old and New Testaments cohesively? Can you think of some examples of places in the New Testament where the writer drew on the Old Testament?**

The account of Philip and the Ethiopian in Acts 8:26–40 provides an excellent example of this cohesion. The Ethiopian was reading from the Old Testament book of Isaiah, yet he did not know to whom it applied. So, Philip had to speak to the man about the Gospel—about Jesus.

The Old Testament was like a pencil drawing, a piece of art begun but not completed. It still needed hues and colors. Any ambiguity in the Old Testament is developed in the New Testament, as the New Testament finishes the whole drawing by filling in the needed hues and colors.

So, the Old and New Testaments are not two books but one. Therefore, one can truly understand the Old Testament only in the light of the New Testament and its testimony of Christ. The reverse also holds true; one cannot really understand Jesus Christ until one knows the Old Testament. Again, the Old and New Testaments are not two books but one.

Is it true that you can make the Bible prove anything and that it's all a matter of interpretation?

If there is one Bible, why are there so many different interpretations? How is it possible for three people to read the same passage of the Bible and have three different interpretations? And how should we interpret the Bible? The answer is found in three simple words: context, context, context!

1. Before we dive in, consider the movies you watch and the books you read. What genre are they usually? How does your mood affect your choice of book or movie, and vice versa?

The genre sets the context in which you understand the movie or book. The same can be said about the Bible. The Bible contains sixty-six books. However, not all sixty-six books are in the same genre.

2. So, how do we interpret the Bible? One way is by paying attention to the genre. Using pieces of paper, bookmark each of the passages below in your Bible. Then read the passages and write down which genre each one belongs to.

- 2 Kings 18:1–3: ....
- Psalm 23: ....
- Proverbs 20:19: ....
- Jeremiah 23:5–6: ....
- Acts 2:22–24: ....
- Matthew 5:43–48: ....
- Luke 8:4–8: ....
- 1 Corinthians 1:1–3: ....

Each of the passages above are different in both form and purpose! Historical narratives and poetic verses differ greatly. Parables (stories meant to teach a point) must be interpreted differently than wisdom literature. In other words, the context of the literary form (i.e., the genre) matters. Just as it doesn't make sense to laugh at a tragic movie, it doesn't make sense to read a psalm of praise as if it's a historical narrative. Literary form matters just as much as the context of time, setting, people, and places in which the Scripture was written. To ignore a particular verse's genre when interpreting is to ignore its context. And when context is ignored, misinterpretations happen.

In addition to genre, we also pay attention to the purpose of a given text—whether it is prescriptive or descriptive. For example, consider the books of Acts and Romans. Romans is considered a prescriptive book; it prescribes what is and what should be. However, Acts is descriptive; it describes the events as they occurred, some good and some bad. So, we cannot read the history of the church in the book of Acts and try to make the modern church how it was in the first century. That is not the purpose of Acts. The book of Romans prescribes and shapes the modern church. The book of Acts describes and shares about the ancient church.

3. Have you ever read the same Bible passage as another person but come away with different ideas about its meaning? When you have questions about a passage, where do you turn to find clarity?

....

....

....

A sure way to misunderstand the Bible is to ask, "What does this verse mean to *me*?" When we do so, we forget that the meaning of Scripture belongs to the author, not the person reading the Bible. When we read the Bible, we must consider the genre and purpose, the context around the specific passage, and the context of the Bible as a whole. Since the Bible is God-breathed (see 2 Timothy 3:16–17), we can also rely on other verses in the Bible to provide further insight into what a particular text is saying. This method—using Scripture passages that speak clearly on a topic to interpret other passages on the topic that are less clear—is called using a proof text, or a chair passage.

4. **Let's see this in action. Flip through the book of Revelation and examine the content. What content do you see? What genre is the book? Do you find it confusing?**

5. **Now look at 1 Thessalonians 4:13–5:11. What topic is it discussing? What genre is it? How might this help us determine whether any given interpretation of the book of Revelation is correct?**

Because the Bible has one author, we can count on the clearer passages of Scripture to interpret the less clear passages. The clear words about the end times in 1 Thessalonians help us understand the less clear imagery, symbolism, numbers, and visions of Revelation.

6. **Let's take a look at a few other chair passages—sections of the Bible that treat certain doctrines at length. Read the passages below. Which doctrine or topic does each passage teach on?**

- **Genesis 3:**
- **Romans 3:21–26:**
- **1 Corinthians 10:14–22:**

So, there are sections throughout the Bible that robustly teach about a particular subject, which means that these passages must be respected when reading other passages that are less clear on the same subject.

7. **How can we read the Bible as Jesus and the New Testament read it? Let's consider the book of Jonah. Some people interpret the whole account as an allegory—symbolic or abstract. Read Jonah 1:1–3. What details in these verses indicate that this is not an allegory but rather a historical account?**

8. **Now read Luke 11:29–30. How does Jesus reference Jonah? Does He speak of Jonah as if the account were a metaphor?**

9. **Likewise, consider how Paul speaks about Abraham, the Law, and Jesus in Galatians 3:15–29. Does he act like they are fictitious, theoretical, or symbolic? How does he speak about them?**

Great problems arise when our handling and interpretations of the Scriptures differ from that of Jesus and His apostles. How can we view Jonah as an allegorical character when Jesus views him as a historical character? Both views can't be right! Furthermore, how is it possible to diminish key Old and New Testament doctrines when Paul highlights them in his teaching to Christians in the first century?

The goal in reading, interpreting, preaching, and confessing the Bible is to read, interpret, preach, and confess the Bible like Jesus and His apostles. When our reading, interpreting, preaching, and confessing do not sound like Jesus and His apostles, we have created great confusion and placed our interpretations above the authority of God's Holy Word.

10. What is the overarching story of the Bible? To answer this, let's see what Scripture says.

- **Where does Paul turn when explaining the Scriptures in Acts 17:2–3?**

- **How does Jesus interpret Moses and the Prophets in Luke 24:27?**

- **What is the central theme of the Gospel books according to John 20:31?**

- **What is the central theme of the Epistles according to 1 Corinthians 2:2?**

We might wonder if the whole Bible is limited to the theme of Christ's birth, life, death, and resurrection. Is the Bible constricted to Christ exclusively? But we must recognize that upholding the centrality of Christ in the story of the Bible does not negate other biblical themes. The Christian can certainly read, understand, and converse over themes such as creation, original sin, the church, the end times, sin, the devil, the world, pagan idolatry, and the like. However, we understand everything under the supremacy of Christ. As we discuss the many different themes of the Bible, we do so in light of Christ, who is the Alpha and Omega.

11. Whenever we read the Bible (or take in any information), we do so with presuppositions—ways of seeing the world, emotional states, political allegiances, physical environments, social conditioning, intelligence, cultural values. How might these things distort our reading of the Bible? What attitudes or perceptions do we have that could affect our reading of the Bible?

12. **So, what can I do to understand the Bible better? Take a look at the opening of many of Paul's letters: Romans 1:7; 1 Corinthians 1:2; Galatians 1:2; Ephesians 1:1; Philippians 1:1; Colossians 1:2; and 1 Thessalonians 1:1. Who are these letters addressed to? Who would have heard the letters?**

To understand the Bible and understand it better, we must read it with the church. While personal, devotional study of God's Word is beneficial, it is equally important—if not more important—to read, mark, and inwardly digest God's Holy Word together with a local church. Often, in the local church and under the guidance of a pastor, our political allegiances, emotional states, social conditioning, and other presuppositions will be hedged by others as we hear from the Bible together.

Are there a lot of mistakes in the Bible?

One common misconception, particularly from uninformed critics, is that the Bible is full of mistakes. While critics often fail to expound on what they mean by this statement, nonetheless, it serves the Christian to boldly explore this idea with academic intrigue. Let's do so by asking some important questions.

Did you know that we have over five thousand surviving manuscripts of the New Testament? Did you know that we do not have the *original* manuscripts of the Old and New Testaments, the ones as they were first written by the apostles and other writers? That is right. We only have copies.

1. **If we only have copies, can we really trust the Bible? The short answer is yes, absolutely, but let's do some math about historical documents to show why. When did Plato live and write? When were the earliest copies we have of his writings made? (Look this up on the internet.) How many years are there between the two?**

....

....

....

....

There are less than a hundred years between some of the original writings of the New Testament and our earliest copies! Plus, we have over five thousand surviving copies of the New Testament. To put that in perspective, we have only several dozen surviving copies of the writings of Plato, Aristotle, and other ancient philosophers. The Bible has the greatest manuscript support of any document from ancient history.

We can trust the Bible, not only because it has great manuscript support, but also because Scripture will endure forever (see Isaiah 40:8). Indeed, Scripture cannot be broken (see John 10:35) and is God-breathed (see 2 Timothy 3:16–17)—it does not have its origins in the will of man, but men spoke from God as they were carried along by the Holy Spirit (see 2 Peter 1:21).

2. **What are variant readings? To find out, let's have some fun. Grab your Bible, look up John 5:4, and read it. Did you have any issues?**

....

....

....

....

If you had trouble finding it, you're not alone. That verse is a textual variant—that is, a text included in some of the Bible manuscripts but not in others. More specifically, John 5:4 is not in some of the oldest manuscripts that we have available. Keep in mind that manuscripts were all copied by hand; scribes would copy a book letter by letter, line by line. No printing presses or copy machines existed. And so, with the thousands upon thousands of manuscripts, lines, and words, there were some occasions when misspellings or accidental switches in word order occurred. Also, there were times when a scribe would take the liberty of adding a short explanation to manuscripts. This would be similar to how we have footnotes in our study Bible or a parenthetical note in a book to explain important background or contextual ideas. Because we have so many Bible manuscripts available to us, we can easily compare them to identify variants and arrive at the author's original wording.

3. **Read John 5:1–9 in the King James Version of the Bible, which includes verse 4. (Or read your own translation if verse 4 is included in the footnotes.) Why might someone have added this passage?**

....

....

....

When this verse was added and by whom we may never know. However, we know that it was added, which is why many translations omit it from the Gospel of John. And so it is worth noting here that any mistakes in translating and any failures in copying should be ascribed not to God's Holy Word but to the person making the translation or copying error.

However, relatively speaking, the copyist mistakes are few, and they do not affect any major doctrine of the Bible, especially doctrines that teach about our salvation. Furthermore, copyist errors are often easily reconciled when closely examined. Thus, we can say with great confidence that God's own Word is truth; it is without error. Indeed, Scripture cannot be broken.

4. **Do you speak more than one language? Have you ever had to translate for someone else or needed someone to translate for you? What are some of the challenges involved in translating?**

....

....

....

....

The Bible is written in three different languages. The Old Testament was written in Hebrew and Aramaic, and the New Testament was written in Koine Greek. Some challenges when translating these languages into English include the word order and sentence structure. For example, Hebrew and Aramaic are written and read right to left. In Koine Greek, the sentence structure is not always the same as in English.

There are two ways to go about any translation project: word for word or thought for thought. Word-for-word translations try to stick as close as possible to the wording of the original text. Thought-for-thought translations attempt to translate the meaning of the original text in a way that sounds natural in the translated language.

5. **Read John 3:16. Then read below the extreme examples of how the two styles of translation might translate that verse. What are some of the drawbacks and positives of each style? Do the translations change the meaning of the Bible?**

- **"Thus for loved God the world, that the Son, the begotten, He gave, that everyone believing in Him may not perish but have life eternal."**
- **"How much did God love the world? He loved the world so much that He gave His only Son. He did this so that everyone faithing in Jesus would not be destroyed but have life forever."**

Good translators try to mediate this tension—sticking to the original language while at the same time making sure the original thoughts of the text are clearly communicated. Some translations do this better than others. For those who don't know the original languages of the Bible, it can be helpful to read several different trusted translations. Even a loose paraphrase version, while not usually recommended for exclusive use, can sometimes help with passages that are difficult to understand grammatically. A faithful pastor can help you determine which translations should be used. There are many excellent and faithful translations that accurately deliver the Word of God in the English language.

The Bible matters because it is the Word of God. The Word of God is not on the same level as other words. It differs from tabloids, self-help books, and motivational speeches because God's Word is inspired. The Holy Spirit gives strength, power, and ability through the Word.

The Word also grants you confidence. Without the Word, you are left digging around inside your emotions, thoughts, and ego for something to hold on to. But through the Word, the God of the universe speaks to you and delivers to you the forgiveness of sins in Christ.

And as a church? Without the Word, the church is susceptible to the crazy ideas of the world that go as fast as they come. Without the Word, we cannot learn from our hearts or feelings about the forgiveness of sins. But with the Word, the church is set upon a rock—the true, abiding rock on which the church can rest with certainty. Without the Word, the church is throwing air to the wind; with the Word, the gates of Hades will never prevail.

Closing Prayer

> *O Lord, may I abide always by Your Word. Lead me not by my own understanding but conform me to Your will, give me discernment, and grant me confidence by Your Holy Word. In the name of Jesus. Amen.*

ABOUT BELIEF

MISCONCEPTIONS ABOUT BELIEF

- **Intellectual assent to the main teachings of Scripture is what makes you a member of the Holy Christian Church.**
- **We cooperate with the Holy Spirit in our conversion.**
- **Our love for God is the motive for all we do in our Christian lives.**

Opening Prayer

Holy Spirit, You inspired the writing of the Scriptures so that we might believe in Jesus, and that by believing, we would have life in His name. As we begin this chapter on faith and belief, keep our eyes fixed on Jesus, the founder and perfecter of our faith, for He has died yet lives and reigns with You and the Father, one God, now and forever. In Jesus' name. Amen.

Introduction

What does it mean to believe in Jesus?

The Bible references faith hundreds of times. Each week, millions of people gather together and confess their faith in Jesus. Yet what we believe, how we believe, and the hoped for results of our belief differ among the many and various congregations throughout the world.

Where I live, in the Bay Area of California, many churches permanently closed during or as a result of the COVID-19 pandemic. This meant thousands of Christians were looking for new church homes. I have had the great honor of walking with many Christians as they looked for a new congregation. As I walked together with these people through the beliefs of our congregation, I found two common threads of questions frequently arose. These common threads include the following: the relationship between the mind and the heart in matters of faith, and the emphasis on God's work or my own work, both in faith's inception and in the daily life of following Jesus.

Questions regarding faith almost always spring from a deeper question regarding assurance of salvation for ourselves or our loved ones. In this session, we will look at such questions regarding faith where misconceptions commonly arise, offering a Lutheran perspective on faith regarding God's role and our role. But most important, our aim is to point ourselves and others toward Jesus for assurance.

Does intellectual assent to the main teachings of Scripture make you a member of the Holy Christian Church?

A common misconception among many Christians is that faith is merely a matter of knowledge and general agreement. If a person intellectually agrees with most of the main teachings of the Bible, does that make him or her a Christian? How many of the main teachings of the Scriptures must be agreed to in order to constitute membership in the one holy Christian and apostolic church? What's the threshold? How much is enough?

When it comes to matters of assurance regarding salvation, as Lutherans, we look to Jesus and the promises of His Word. So, let's dig into some related questions and what the Scriptures have to say in answer.

Let's consider the question "How is intellectual assent different from faith or trust?"

1. **How are you with airplanes? Do you enjoy flying, or does it make you nervous? Have you ever met someone who refused to fly on an airplane?**

Statistically speaking, one's chances of dying in a plane crash, particularly on a commercial airline, are astronomically small. Despite the data, plenty of people refuse to fly. Such people almost certainly know the statistics involved. It probably comes up every time they reveal their distaste for flying. Imagine somebody trying to be helpful by sharing this anecdote: "You know, statistically, you're more likely to die in the car on the way to the airport than in a plane crash."

Intellectually, a person who refuses to fly may know the data. He understands his chances of safety are nearly a guarantee. He doesn't disbelieve or doubt the numbers. But if he refuses to travel by plane, we could confidently say that he does not *trust* airplane travel.

Intellectually, he assents to the safety of airplane travel, but his actions show his distrust, his lack of faith.

As you read through the New Testament, particularly the Gospels, take note of the times when faith is mentioned. When Jesus speaks of faith (or lack of faith), it is often connected to words and actions that reveal the deep trust (or lack of trust) people show in Jesus. Belief limited to knowledge or intellectual agreement without trust is of little value. The enemies of Jesus showcase such untrusting belief.

2. **Read James 2:19. What does James argue here about belief?**

3. **We see James's argument confirmed in the Gospels. Read Mark 1:23–24. What do the demons confess about Jesus? But do they trust Him?**

Another text that often brings confusion concerning the relationship between intellectual agreement and trust is Romans 10:9, where Paul writes, "If you confess with your mouth that Jesus is Lord and believe in your heart that God raised Him from the dead, you will be saved."

This sounds like a pretty straightforward formula. Confess "Jesus is Lord," believe Jesus is risen from the dead, and all is well. But what does it mean to confess and believe Jesus is our resurrected Lord?

4. **Read Philippians 2:9–11. What does Paul say will happen? Based on the passages we read earlier about Jesus' enemies, does this mean every being will trust in Jesus?**

These enemies of Jesus are well aware Jesus is risen from the dead, and it fills them with rage. They will indeed call Jesus "Lord," but only through grinding, gnashing teeth.

So, we see that intellectual assent, general agreement with even the most important teaching of Scripture—the resurrection of the dead—does not automatically save or produce trust in Jesus.

But this is not only a concern for demonic forces. In the Sermon on the Mount, Jesus says,

> **Not everyone who says to Me, "Lord, Lord," will enter the kingdom of heaven, but the one who does the will of My Father who is in heaven. On that day many will say to Me, "Lord, Lord, did we not prophesy in Your name, and cast out demons in Your name, and do many mighty works in Your name?" And then will I declare to them, "I never knew you; depart from Me, you workers of lawlessness." (Matthew 7:21–23)**

For some, calling Jesus "Lord" is no confession of faith. For some, calling Jesus "Lord" is a means to an end, a way to gain power, fame, and glory. Let's consider two stories in the book of Acts.

5. Read Acts 8:9–24. Why did Simon the magician seek the Holy Spirit? What happened to him?

Also consider the sons of Sceva. In Acts 19, these itinerant Jewish exorcists heard Paul was doing extraordinary miracles, so they decided to use Paul's formula, so to speak. As they encountered an evil spirit, they invoked the name of the Lord Jesus, saying, "I adjure you by the Jesus whom Paul proclaims" (v. 13). But the evil spirit responded right back, "Jesus I know, and Paul I recognize, but who are you?" (v. 15). The sons of Sceva were routed by this evil spirit and ran away naked and bleeding.

Still there are numerous examples of faithful people in the New Testament who put their trust in Jesus as Lord.

6. Read Mark 5:25–34. In contrast to the motivations in the previous accounts, how did this woman's actions reveal her faith? How did Jesus respond? What was the result?

We see similar stories with the Samaritan leper who returned to thank Jesus (Luke 17:11–19), as well as Bartimaeus, who was blind and received his sight (Mark 10:46–52). We learn from these examples that those who call on the Lord and are saved reveal their faith through deep trust, through words and actions that look to Jesus as their Lord, and not merely as some tool to be invoked for power.

So, if general agreement with the teachings of the Bible is not our passport into the church, then what is?

Let's return to the airplane discussion. If you board a plane and it takes you from one destination to another, how much credit can you take for getting the plane from one destination to the other? Pretty much none. The plane would have flown with or without you.

In faith, it is much the same. We can claim no credit for the Holy Spirit delivering us from the domain of darkness to the kingdom of light, the kingdom of Jesus.

Three interconnected things are involved as a person becomes part of the church. They are (in no particular order) God's Word, Baptism, and the Holy Spirit.

7. **Let's take a look at what happens on Pentecost as an example. Read Acts 2. What role did the Holy Spirit play in this event? How was God's Word proclaimed? What do the people gathered do in response to Peter's proclamation of Christ?**

....

....

....

....

....

Notice how God's Word, the Holy Spirit, and Baptism all play a role in these three thousand people being added to the church. The Holy Spirit inspires those speaking. The Holy Spirit makes it possible for them to proclaim God's mighty works. The Holy Spirit enables them to speak in this language that everyone understands. The Word cuts those hearing to the heart and offers them the remedy of forgiveness and life that comes through Baptism.

As I mentioned before, the order is not particular. The Holy Spirit works where and when and how He chooses. Sometimes it is the Word of God proclaimed that brings people to faith in Jesus. Sometimes it is the written Word of God in the Scriptures. And sometimes it is the Word of God in and with water in Baptism that serves as the entrance point into the kingdom of God and the Body of Christ.

8. **Read the following passages about Baptism. Who is active in these passages? Do we do the saving?**

- **Titus 3:4–7:**
- **1 Peter 3:21:**

In the Lutheran tradition (as well as many others), people of all ages are able to be baptized. In some traditions, Baptism is only offered to people when they reach a certain age. While another session will cover the Sacraments in more detail, it is worth noting here how our entering into the one holy Christian and apostolic church is passive. The Holy Spirit, present in God's living and active Word, does the work. Whether we are infants, toddlers, teenagers, or adults, God is the one at work in Baptism. We are recipients of God's good gifts in Baptism. These are not gifts we must earn or be a certain age to receive.

In the end, belief in Jesus is sure and certain, not because of us who believe in Him, but because of the one we believe in. Jesus is the most sure and certain thing in the world. He is trustworthy. His promises always become reality, even His promise to rise from the grave. He is far more certain even than the safety of air travel. Moreover, the promised destination of the new creation is far better than any destination an airplane might take you to here in the fallen creation.

Belief in Jesus, trust in Jesus, faith in Jesus, following Jesus lead us to the resurrection of the dead and eternal life in the joys of paradise.

Do we cooperate with the Holy Spirit at all in our conversion?

In the previous section, we talked about how faith in Jesus differs from general agreement with the Bible's teachings. In this section, we will address our role in coming to faith, our role in conversion. What is our role? We are recipients. The Holy Spirit creates and sustains faith through God's Word and Sacraments. As Martin Luther writes in the Small Catechism regarding the Apostles' Creed,

> **I believe that I cannot by my own reason or strength believe in Jesus Christ, my Lord, or come to Him; but the Holy Spirit has called me by the Gospel, enlightened me with His gifts, sanctified and kept me in the one true faith. (Third Article)**

We cannot bring ourselves to believe in Jesus. We cannot draw near to Jesus by our own strength or intelligence. As Jesus says, "No one can come to Me unless the Father who sent Me draws him. And I will raise him up on the last day" (John 6:44).

The Father draws us to Jesus through the Holy Spirit's work of calling us by the Gospel. The Holy Spirit brings about our conversion to faith in Jesus by pointing us ever toward Jesus' death and resurrection for our forgiveness, salvation, and eternal life. We are passive recipients of these gifts.

But what about free will? Don't I have to accept Jesus into my heart?

Free will is among the most confusing concepts or doctrines in the Christian faith. The Lutheran Confessions speak to the topic of free will on several occasions. These writings explain how free will exists in everyday matters. We can choose what to eat, where to shop, which career we would like to pursue. But even in these everyday matters, free will is limited. I may wish to be an astronaut or a professional athlete, but those careers may not happen for me, no matter how much effort I exert to make them happen. Our choices have limited freedom. I cannot defy gravity or cause the lottery to pick my ticket's numbers.

But the Scriptures and the Lutheran Confessions show that in matters of salvation, we do not have free will. Indeed, our wills are bound in the opposite direction: toward sin.

1. **Read Romans 7:15–20. Why is Paul frustrated in this passage? What does Paul imply about his will? To what is Paul held captive? What does this tell us about ourselves?**

....

....

....

....

....

We will all fall short at times because sin dwells within each of us. And though our sins of the past and future are forgiven by Jesus' sacrificial death on the cross, we remain captive in these fallen, sinful bodies of death. We need new bodies, which Jesus will give when He returns and raises the dead.

We cannot stop sinning. Our free will is never free enough to live perfect lives. We are bound to fall short of God's glory. We cannot save ourselves.

What's worse, we are not only captive to sin, we are dead in our sins. And being dead in our sins, we have no capacity in and of ourselves to believe in Jesus, to accept Him. Because dead things and dead people don't and can't do anything.

But what does it mean to be dead in our trespasses and sins?

2. **Let's turn to Paul again. Read Romans 6:23. How did we earn death?**

Jesus tells a parable about a servant who owed his king ten thousand talents. A single talent was equal to about twenty years' wages. This servant somehow has managed to amass a debt that would take him 200,000 years to work off. He pleads with the king, "Have patience with me, and I will pay you everything" (Matthew 18:26).

This parable illustrates what it looks like to be dead under the weight of sin. If we think we can somehow manage to pull ourselves out and earn our way back into God's favor, we are just as delusional as this servant thinking he could pay off more money than he would earn in several thousand lifetimes.

Swedish pastor and novelist Bo Giertz's most well-known work is called *The Hammer of God*. In it, Giertz tells several fictional stories related to pastoral care. In one such story, Giertz records a conversation between two pastors. One is young and quite new to the role. The other is a more seasoned veteran. The younger pastor makes a pious comment about how he has given his heart to Jesus. The veteran pastor compares one's heart to a rusty tin can on a garbage heap. It's not worth giving to anyone. Yet God in His mercy stoops down and picks up the tin can, rescues it, and brings it home.

Giertz's story showcases our standing before God. We are like rusty tin cans on garbage heaps with no way of escaping on our own.

3. **That story brings to life Paul's words in Ephesians 2:4–5. Read that passage now. How do these words give hope to us rusty cans? What does it tell us about our initial conversion and coming to faith? Who alone is the active agent in bringing us to faith?**

4. **Now turn to Ezekiel 37:3–6. Again, who is acting in this incredible account? What must happen to us dry bones to have any hope of life?**

The following question often arises: If the Holy Spirit works through God's Word and Sacraments to create and sustain faith, and we are passive recipients, why do some people *not* come to faith in Jesus after hearing or reading God's Word?

Yes, there are plenty of people who hear God's Word and refuse to receive God's Word. Indeed, there are plenty of people who are baptized and come to reject the promises of their Baptism. Somehow, paradoxically, people are passive in their reception of God's promises given through His Word yet often active in their refusal and rejection of God's Word.

Here's an example that may help. There's this hilarious moment in the film *Little Giants*, an underdog story about an undersized youth football team. In the early stages of the movie, a wide receiver for the team, Rashid "Hot Hands" Hanon, is on the receiving end of a pass. Most football receptions are very active. Receivers must maneuver and reach and catch and hold on to the pass.

But Hanon's reception in this case involved the football being lodged into his helmet and stuck there.

That is how we receive salvation. That is how we receive faith. It is given. We might be doing anything or nothing, when out of nowhere, the Holy Spirit calls us by the Gospel.

5. **Paul's own conversion is a great example of this. Turn to Acts 9:1–19. What happened to Paul on the road? What was the result?**

Likewise, consider those people gathered at Pentecost in Acts 2. There are dozens of examples in the book of Acts alone of this happening.

Yet there are others who hear the exact same Word of the Gospel and reject it. The Gospel was given like a football lodged in their helmet, but they swatted it out and kicked it as far away as possible. Yes, we can by all means reject the Holy Spirit and throw away the Gospel.

After the Holy Spirit calls us by the Gospel and we come to faith, we have responsibilities to remain faithful, but that initial gift of faith is given by the Holy Spirit through God's Word and Sacraments. Faith is not received by some acrobatic, athletic feat on our part. We're not Justin Jefferson or Jerry Rice or Franco Harris making some immaculate reception of faith. Rather, it is the Holy Spirit who is responsible for bringing us to faith through God's Word.

6. **Jesus tells a story that speaks to this; it's known as the parable of the sower. Let's read that now from Matthew 13:1–9. Does this parable make sense to you upon first reading? What is strange about the farmer's methods?**

7. **It didn't make sense to Jesus' disciples at first either. Now read Matthew 13:18–23, where Jesus explains the meaning of this parable. Who is the farmer with the strange method for scattering seed, and what is He scattering?**

Jesus explains that those who hear, read, or experience God's Word but do not understand it are like seeds planted on a road. Satan comes and snatches away the Word like a bird eating seed off of a road. But this isn't simply a matter of lacking intelligence or knowledge. Jesus quotes the prophet Isaiah, saying, "For this people's heart has grown dull, and with their ears they can barely hear, and their eyes they have closed" (Matthew 13:15).

People who don't understand the Word have hearts that are hardened like asphalt. They have shut their eyes and plugged their ears to the Word. They do not understand because they do not trust the Word, and they do not trust the source of the Word.

8. **Read Acts 7:51–53, where Stephen speaks to the crowd right before they stone him to death. What does this tell us about the possibility of resisting the Holy Spirit? What fruit does the crowd display that speaks to their hard hearts?**

In the end, our lack of cooperation with the Holy Spirit, our passivity in the Holy Spirit's work, is a good thing. If we did cooperate in our conversion, we would be forced to look to ourselves and our own performance for assurance. But we are passive recipients. This means that in looking for assurance of faith, we are not looking to ourselves, but we are ever looking to God—Father and Son and Holy Spirit. We look to the cross, where Jesus defeated sin. We look to the empty tomb, where Jesus defeated death. We look to our Baptism, where God claimed us as His own. We look to God's words and promises that proclaim us forgiven in Jesus.

Is our love for God simply the motive for all we do in our Christian lives?

Thus far, we have walked through how faith in Jesus is all about trusting Him and His promises. We have also looked at how our role in being brought to faith is passive. It is the work of the Holy Spirit.

In our final question for this chapter, we will examine our role in our lives of faith as followers of Jesus.

So, what is our motivation to love God and love others?

1. **Let's start by turning to Scripture. Read Jesus' words in Matthew 22:37–40. What does He call us to in this passage?**

It seems straightforward enough, but there is much confusion surrounding love for God and love for neighbor.

I think many of the misconceptions come from hearing Jesus say this: "If you love Me, you will keep My commandments" (John 14:15). Here is how this plays out unhelpfully. People read this verse and wrongly assume that their love for God will save them. But as we established above, in matters of salvation and eternal life, we are passive. God does the work. God sends Jesus into our world to bear our sin and be our Savior. Jesus died, rose, and is returning for us and our salvation. The Holy Spirit calls us to faith, gives us faith as a gift through the Word and Sacraments. We receive what God gives.

Jesus' words in John 14 are simply telling us the truth. When we keep His Word, we show our love for Him. When we fail to keep His Word, it is sin. We are bound by sin, captive to it. There will be times in our lives when we show our love for Jesus by keeping His Word. There will also be times in our lives when we lack love for Jesus, and this will be shown through our sinfulness.

As we consider this section's question regarding our love for God as motivation for our Christian lives, we must acknowledge that we will not and cannot love God or our neighbors perfectly.

2. Read Hebrews 12:1–2. How does this encourage us? On what do we depend for salvation?

If we look to our own love for God and love for neighbor as the proof of our faith and salvation, we will be constantly worried that we are not doing enough. But if we look to Christ, the founder and perfecter of our faith, we will see there that He and His work are sufficient.

Our love, then, for God and neighbor is out of response to God's love. As the apostle John writes, "We love because He first loved us" (1 John 4:19).

Our motivation is not to secure or earn or even maintain God's love, nor to somehow secure or earn more of God's love (as if that were possible). Our motive for loving others is that we are loved by God, who gave us life and gave us new life in Jesus.

3. Speaking of our new life in Jesus, have you heard or read the term *sanctification*? Do you know what it means?

At its most basic definition, *sanctification* means "to make something or someone holy." Considering what we have covered thus far, you perhaps can rightly see that sanctification is God's responsibility. Jesus makes us holy by dying for our sins. However, sanctification is not a one-time event.

4. **Can you think of some ways the Holy Spirit makes us holy?**

Jesus says to His apostles after His resurrection,

> **"Peace be with you. As the Father has sent Me, even so I am sending you." And when He had said this, He breathed on them and said to them, "Receive the Holy Spirit. If you forgive the sins of any, they are forgiven them; if you withhold forgiveness from any, it is withheld." (John 20:21–23)**

This vocation of forgiving sins is gifted to the church, and the church calls and entrusts this sacred vocation to pastors. The Holy Spirit is continually at work, calling and gathering us for worship, where we are made holy in absolution.

Likewise with the Lord's Supper, after eating the meal, Jesus says to His apostles, "Do this in remembrance of Me" (Luke 22:19). He entrusts them to carry on this meal as a means of delivering forgiveness, as a way to make His people holy for generations. We participate in the Lord's Supper by taking and eating, taking and drinking.

Sanctification is something we receive, but the Holy Spirit produces good works in us. We are set apart as God's sacred people in Baptism, called to adorn ourselves in good works throughout our lives of faith. We are called to seek good and abstain from evil.

5. **Read Colossians 3:12–14. How does Paul describe the sanctified life of the Christian?**

This is our role as God's people. We practice compassion, kindness, humility, meekness, and patience. We forgive one another as we have been forgiven. We love our neighbors and seek to live in harmony with all.

No, we will never do these things perfectly. The Holy Spirit is perfect in His work, but we are still sinners and will remain so until Jesus returns and ushers in the new creation.

As we follow Jesus, we are like seeds that are planted, grow, blossom, and bear fruit. We often focus our attention on the benefits of following Jesus in the future. When Jesus returns and raises the dead, He will bring those who trust in Him into eternal life in the new creation. That is our future hope and the greatest benefit one could imagine.

But are there more earthly benefits to following Jesus?

Yes, but we must be careful in addressing these. Since before Jesus was born, preachers and prophets have sought to proclaim a false word of God that promises wealth and ease in this life.

6. **What are some false promises you've heard made? Who are these false promises often conditional upon?**

....

....

....

....

....

The earthly benefits we receive from following Jesus have nothing to do with increased material possessions or lives that are objectively easier. Jesus tells us how God "makes His sun rise on the evil and on the good, and sends rain on the just and on the unjust" (Matthew 5:45).

Likewise, we see throughout the Scriptures that suffering is a part of life, especially for the Christian. For those who trust Jesus, though, we have peace with God. When we face the sufferings of this world, we enter into the counterintuitive process of rejoicing in our sufferings, knowing that suffering produces endurance, endurance produces character, and character produces hope, and hope in Jesus never puts us to shame (see Romans 5:1–5).

The personal benefit of faith in Jesus cannot be measured with concrete, objective criteria. In the end, trusting Jesus means we become more and more like Jesus. We become more loving, more patient, more compassionate, more generous, more hospitable. We become less fearful, less hurried, less indifferent, less stingy, less prejudiced.

And though these things will be true, I hesitate to write them, lest anyone focus their attention on these external markers rather than on Jesus Himself. If we look at ourselves for assurance that we truly have faith, we will be forever filled with doubt. For we will always find ourselves lacking in love and filled with fear. We will never have done enough to look to ourselves and be truly certain of our faith.

But if we look to Jesus, we will see the founder and perfecter of our faith. We will see the cross and empty tomb of the one whom we can trust. We will see the lengths of love He went to in order to rescue and redeem us, just as the promises and prophecies of God's Word declare to us.

The fruit of our faith (becoming more loving, patient, and like Jesus) is certainly a benefit to us, but who might benefit even more from the faith and love of my Christian life?

Often it is our neighbors who benefit far more. How much richer is a friendship marked by compassion rather than indifference? How much more joyful is a family filled with generosity than stuck in stinginess? How much more beautiful is a congregation that shows hospitality than one that shuts people out in prejudice?

7. **Consider some of the Christian friends, family members, or mentors in your life. How have their lives of faith and love been a blessing to you? As you are willing, share some stories of the blessing of Christians displaying the fruit of faith to you or others.**

The fruit of our faith is something our neighbors will delight in. And we pray that the Holy Spirit would utilize the fruit of our faith to plant and grow the seeds of faith in others so that more people would come to trust in Jesus and His saving words of eternal life.

Our Christian lives of faith are lives of response to God's love. In love, God has forgiven our sin through Jesus' death on the cross. In love, God has destroyed death by Jesus' resurrection. In love, God has sent Jesus to defeat Satan and cast him out of our presence forever. In love, God has sent the Holy Spirit to call us to faith in Jesus by the power of this Good News.

Closing Prayer

> *Jesus, You have kept all Your promises and proven Yourself trustworthy. Strengthen us to love and forgive others, as You have loved and forgiven us so that our lives might be an echo of You and Your words of eternal life, for You live and reign with the Father and the Holy Spirit, one God, evermore and evermore. Amen.*

SESSION 5

ABOUT THE CHURCH

MISCONCEPTIONS ABOUT THE CHURCH

- **The church is a human institution put together by human beings.**
- **The church should stress fellowship more and doctrine less.**
- **We go to church primarily to get something out of it.**

Opening Prayer

Lord God, You find, gather, and forgive Your wayward creatures through Your divinely established church. Bless and sustain the church through Your Word and Sacraments so that Your mission of salvation in Christ Jesus can extend to the ends of the earth. Amen.

Introduction

Roughly how many churches are within a five-mile radius of your home? Roughly how many churches are within a twenty-mile radius of your home? What do those churches have in common? What makes them different from one another?

You may live in the city or the country. Your community might be densely packed with people, or it may have more cows than humans. You may live in North America somewhere within the Sun Belt, the Corn Belt, the Rust Belt, or the Bible Belt. You may live in Africa or Europe.

Just as there are endless differences in the places that we call home, churches come in all shapes and sizes, confessions and varieties. Some churches are growing, while others are shrinking. Some churches are newly formed, while others have been around for centuries. We can find churches that have pipe organs and pianos, or others that have guitars and drums.

All of these different churches—and all the differences between them—raise many questions. Are churches merely human institutions, like a grocery store or a coffee shop? Is the church a gathering of like-minded people who are passionate about weak coffee and judging others? Is the church a place for entertainment, or is there something more going on here?

Is the church a human institution put together by human beings?

This is a big question. To help us answer this, we will rely on the 5W1H method journalists use to report stories and police use to conduct investigations: Who? What? Where? When? Why? How?

1. **What happens when someone wants to open a coffee shop or automotive repair garage? Is this how the church works too?**

But is the church a human institution akin to a coffee shop or an automotive repair garage? Do human beings establish the church? Does God have a part to play in establishing the church? To put it directly, *who* forms the church? Finding an answer to this question will take us to the beginning—the *very* beginning of all things in Genesis.

2. **Read Genesis 3:8–10. What are Adam and Eve doing? What is God doing?**

Seeking His wayward creatures with the love and compassion of a parent looking for a lost child, God comes to find Adam and Eve. His question—"Where are you?"—is not inflected with retribution or scorn, but rather love and concern. God embarks on a mission to find, gather, and forgive sinners.

God's mission went well beyond the Garden of Eden. After finding Adam and Eve (and winning the first game of hide-and-seek), God promises that He will send a Savior to undo all that had been done (Genesis 3:15). God's mission to find, gather, and forgive goes well beyond the book of Genesis. Throughout the rest of the Old Testament, we hear about God actively finding, gathering, and forgiving His people.

3. **Let's look at a few examples. Read each passage below and discuss what God is doing for His people in it.**

- **Exodus 3:7–10:**
- **Deuteronomy 7:6–8:**
- **Jeremiah 31:31–32:**

4. **The ministry of Jesus in the New Testament continues the divine mission to find, gather, and forgive sinners. How do the following passages continue this theme?**

- **Luke 19:10:**

- **Matthew 23:37:**

- **John 15:16:**

From the beginning, God has been asking, "Where are you?" as He goes about His mission to find, gather, and forgive His people. God has gathered a people—a people called out of the darkness and into the light—and established His church. Jesus made it clear whose church it is when He said, "I will build *My* church, and the gates of hell shall not prevail against it" (Matthew 16:18, emphasis added).

Who, therefore, forms the church? God forms the church. The one holy Christian and apostolic church is a divine institution created, sustained, and built by the Father, the Son, and the Holy Spirit. God's mission to find, gather, and forgive His people takes shape in the divine establishment of the church.

Does this mean that humans have no part to play in establishing congregations? Not exactly. As we explore this question further—what is the visible church and how is it formed?—we will come to find that God uses ordinary people to accomplish His extraordinary work of finding, gathering, and forgiving people.

In answering the question of who, we have also stumbled on the answer to why. Who forms the church? God forms the church. Why does God form the church? To satisfy the question that He asked Adam and Eve in the garden after sin entered into creation. Ever since the fall of humanity, God has been on a mission to find, gather, and forgive sinners. Every single Christian congregation is like a big sign from God asking, "Where are you?" Every local congregation is an outpost for God calling sinners out of hiding and into God's grace and mercy. Wherever the Word is proclaimed and the Sacraments are rightly administered, God is at work covering His people in the promises of Jesus and not measly fig leaves. This is why God has formed the church.

We have explored how God (who) establishes the church to find, gather, and forgive sinners (why). Yet there are still many more questions and misconceptions about the church. Where exactly is the church? And what do we mean when we say "the church"?

5. **Read Revelation 7:9–17, a passage that will begin to answer these questions. Around what or whom is this great multitude gathering?**

.....

.....

.....

.....

.....

The Revelation passage is a glimpse into the kingdom of heaven. You could say that this is a peek into the church in eternity, or what people sometimes call the church triumphant.

6. **Does that mean that the church is only in heaven? Not so fast. Look closer at verses 9–10. From where does this great multitude come?**

.....

.....

.....

.....

.....

Where, then, is the church to be found? In heaven and on earth. Those who gather around the Lamb—Christ Jesus—gather both in heaven and on earth. This means that the church is composed of those who have already died and, through faith in Christ Jesus, been numbered among the great multitude gathered around the throne of the Lamb. The Bible tells us that this is "so great a cloud of witnesses" (Hebrews 12:1). This means that the church is also composed of those who are still on their earthly pilgrimages living by faith in Christ Jesus. By the power of the Holy Spirit, the church on earth gathers around the Word of God and the sacramental gifts that God has given to His church. On earth, the church gathers in a multitude of places and congregational settings: urban and rural, large and small, old and new. Yet like the church in heaven, the church on earth gathers around the Lamb, Christ Jesus.

If where the church is found includes heaven and earth, then what do we mean when we say "the church"? While we cannot see the church that is in heaven, we can certainly see many visible churches all around us. We often speak of "the church" in rather vague terms.

7. **Think of the different ways you use the word *church*. What different meanings are attached to it?**

Making sense of these different usages of the same word requires some distinctions.

8. **Look up the following passages. How is Scripture using the word *church* in each of them?**

- **Matthew 16:18–19:**
- **Colossians 1:18:**

When Scripture speaks like this, we often call this the "invisible church," or simply, "the church." The invisible church is all true believers in Christ Jesus—those in heaven and on earth, those who have already died in the faith as well as those who are still living the pilgrimage of faith on earth. We cannot see the invisible church because it requires seeing more than we are capable of seeing: hearts and faith, heaven and what God alone knows and sees—true believers in Christ Jesus.

9. How is Scripture using the word *church* in these passages?

- **Galatians 1:2:**
- **Romans 16:5:**

By this, Scripture is referring to what we call the visible church, which can be seen and encountered here on earth. This includes church buildings and the people within those buildings, as well as various Christian denominations. We can see the visible church all around us. However, the visible church and the invisible church do not automatically overlap. A person may occupy a pew within the visible church but utterly loathe and reject faith in Jesus. This means that the person is part of the visible church but not the invisible church. On the other hand, those who have died in the faith are no longer present within the visible church, but they are part of the invisible church. While human hands may build the visible church (buildings, denominations), God builds and sustains the invisible church.

Thus far, we have discussed who establishes the church (God) and why He establishes the church (to find, gather, and forgive sinners). We have also explored where the church is (heaven and earth) and what the church is (the congregation of saints and true believers in Christ Jesus). We now turn our attention to two final questions: When is the church formed? How is the church formed?

10. Read 1 Corinthians 3:5–9. What do these verses say about how the church is formed? What role do humans have in forming and growing the church? What role does God have in forming and growing the church?

It should be clear by now that "the church" can have several different meanings. Therefore, pinpointing when the church is formed depends on which aspect of the church one has in mind.

For example, if one is thinking of the church as all true believers (the invisible church) formed by God's initiative to find, gather, and forgive sinners, then the church has been around from the beginning. Whenever God made a promise and His people believed Him (e.g., Genesis 15:6), the church was taking shape. Not only did this early form of the church exist in the beginning, but the community of true believers gathered around Christ Jesus will exist in the future as well. The book of Revelation talks about the worship of Christ Jesus persisting forever and ever (see Revelation 4:10). In this regard, the church exists in the when of eternity.

Nevertheless, we can also pinpoint some specific moments as being important in the formation of the visible church.

11. Can you think of any accounts from Scripture that are important to the formation of the visible church?

This leads to the last in our series of 5W1H questions: How is the church formed? Based on the answers to our previous questions, it should be obvious that the church is formed by God. God's mission compels Him to gather a people and form the church. The Word of God, the power of the Holy Spirit, and the sacramental gifts that God has given to His church (Baptism, the Lord's Supper, Absolution) are the powerful means by which God forms the church. These are not humanly manufactured or man-made. God has instituted and implemented these gifts for the formation of His church.

Does that mean that humans have no part in the formation of the church? Far from it! God has given these divine gifts to us so that we can use them in the formation of the church. The human hands of a pastor pour out the water of Baptism as God finds, gathers, and forgives sinners. Human voices proclaim the Word of God and the Good News of the Gospel. God uses us to form the church! When we become a part of the church, our daily life is imbued with power and purpose: God uses us to do the work of finding, gathering, and forgiving sinners. God brings us into His mission, grafts us into His church, and uses us to accomplish His extraordinary work of finding, gathering, and forgiving people.

12. **How have you seen this in action? Who did God use to bring you into His church?**

We began with a relatively simple question: Is the church a human institution put together by human beings? While the answers are not all that complicated, they are somewhat unexpected. This seemingly ordinary thing that we call "church" is mysteriously beautiful. God desires and directs the formation of the church in heaven and on earth, in time and eternity. God has been working to form the church ever since He first asked, "Where are you?" This divinely instituted church comes into being through human hands and voices, efforts and endeavors. God's church—and the local manifestations of it that we see all around us—is a mysteriously beautiful gift of God!

Should the church stress fellowship more and doctrine less?

About fifty years ago, an American funk band named War released a song called "Why Can't We Be Friends?" The song is only about four minutes long, but it repeats the same question forty-five times: Why can't we be friends?

Fifty years later, people are still asking this question. Disunity and dissension abound all around us: people disagree about politics and public policy, culture and media, sports and the weather. It can even seem like strong convictions and confessions of faith cause people to disagree with one another. This prompts some to think like this: If convictions cause people to disagree, then not having convictions will lead to agreement. Why can't we be friends? Because of our beliefs. If we get rid of our beliefs, then friendship will follow. Right?

Not really. This line of thinking treats beliefs, convictions, and confessions of faith as the cause of disunity. Might it be possible that these things do not cause disunity but simply reveal it? What if our beliefs, convictions, and confessions of faith are actually a step closer to unity because we have revealed the fault lines and places of disagreement? What if doctrine helps fellowship rather than hurts it?

1. **Read Matthew 16:13–19. What two questions does Jesus ask the disciples? What is Jesus doing by asking these questions? What do these verses have to say about the relationship between fellowship and doctrine?**

This interchange between Jesus and the disciples raises some questions and concepts to explore. We have been using these two words: *doctrine* and *fellowship*. What does *doctrine* mean? Doctrine is what we believe, teach, and confess about the Christian faith. Doctrine is not dry, dusty dogma invented by churches in order to stifle progress. Rather, doctrine is a lively exposition of truth founded on the living voice of God that is Holy Scripture.

2. **Read Deuteronomy 6:6–9. Based on this description, how does God want His people to engage with His Word?**

God desires for us to believe, teach, and confess His truth. This is doctrine. This is a good thing. But what does doctrine have to do with fellowship? Does it help or hinder our ability to be friends and get along?

As we will discuss, doctrine promotes true and meaningful fellowship. Just as a compass is able to point north and guide wanderers in the right direction, doctrine enables us to orient ourselves in relation to one another and guide us toward true and meaningful fellowship.

3. **In the preface to the Augsburg Confession, we hear about the aim of confession: "Then we may embrace and maintain the future of one pure and true religion under one Christ, doing battle under Him [Psalm 24:8], living in unity and concord in the one Christian Church" (Augsburg Confession, Preface, paragraph 4). So, what is the goal of this confession?**

In other words, this doctrinal confession is an exercise in fellowship!

4. **Consider the two lines of thinking below. Do either of them make sense? What does each reveal about the pre-requisites for unity and concord?**

- **"We have unity and concord even though I don't actually know what you believe, teach, or confess."**

- **"We have unity and concord even though I don't agree with what you believe, teach, or confess."**

Let's apply those lines of thinking to a different context. Suppose someone said, "We have unity and concord when it comes to sports! I believe that soccer is the best sport to play and watch. You believe that Ping-Pong is the best sport to play and watch. Let us now celebrate our sporting fellowship!" That does not work, does it? We hear that and recognize that there is an impasse at the juncture of unity and concord (fellowship) and what is believed (doctrine).

When faced with this impasse, some people try to either broaden or dilute doctrine in order to find a place of doctrinal agreement. Going back to the previous example, people may try to do the following: "We have unity and concord when it comes to sports! We believe that sports are fun to play and watch. Let us now celebrate our sporting fellowship!" While this statement may garner agreement, it is not really saying much of anything. Such a general assertion is hard to deny. This statement is so much broader and diluted from its original form that it is easy to accept . . . and easy to ignore. Broad and diluted doctrines make for flimsy fellowship.

5. **Read Acts 15:1–5, 22–35. How did the early church rely on doctrine to create fellowship?**

6. **As this Acts passage illustrates, the early church relied on doctrine as the scaffolding for fellowship and unity. According to verse 28, who was responsible for the unity in the church?**

Mysterious as it may sound, the doctrinal agreement and the fellowship of the early church was a co-venture of the Holy Spirit and human members of the church.

This offers some very important insights for us as we seek to address common misconceptions about the church. First, directly confronting doctrinal matters is not a threat to fellowship. Just as exercising strengthens our physical bodies, exercising our ability to discuss and harmonize on doctrinal matters strengthens the Body of Christ that is the church. Though it may be a strenuous conversation, church fellowship and unity are made stronger through the process.

Second, the church does not venture into these matters alone. Instead, the Holy Spirit works in us and through us to promote unity in the church. The Holy Spirit works by fostering humility, gentleness, patience, and love as we engage in the difficult work of doctrinal agreement leading to fellowship. We hear about this in Ephesians 4, as Paul encourages the church to "walk in a manner worthy of the calling to which you have been called, with all humility and gentleness, with patience, bearing with one another in love, eager to maintain the unity of the Spirit in the bond of peace" (Ephesians 4:1–3).

Whether we are looking back in the past to the early church or looking in the present at our own congregations, we can have confidence that doctrine and fellowship complement one another. Rather than sweeping doctrinal disagreements under the rug or acting as if they are inconsequential, we venture into these conversations with humility, gentleness, patience, and love for one another. The Holy Spirit is at work in and through our discussions about the Word of God and confessions of faith. Through it all, we remember that it's not our church anyway. It is God's church, established to find, gather, and forgive sinners.

7. **Now read Ephesians 4:4–6, the verses right after the passage above. Whom do we trust when seeking to establish doctrinal agreement? Whom do we trust when celebrating the unity of fellowship?**

....

....

....

....

....

Though our previous discussion about Acts 15 may make the early church seem like a cornucopia of camaraderie, it was not always joyful unity.

8. **Read 1 Corinthians 1:10–13. What does the Bible say about division in the church? According to these verses, who is the unifying person bringing unity to Paul, Apollos, and Cephas?**

The Bible makes two things very clear when it comes to church unity: (1) Division is not God's desire for the church, and (2) unity is found in Jesus. Understanding both of these points can help us address several misconceptions about the church.

The invisible church (all true believers in Christ Jesus) is not divided. As we confess in the Nicene Creed, there is "one holy Christian and apostolic church." The visible church, on the other hand, is divided in many ways. Some of the divisions that separate the visible church are innocuous and unavoidable. Congregations have geographic divisions, wherein they reside in different states or countries. Different languages and different buildings or gathering spaces also separate the visible church. These unavoidable divisions within the visible church will always exist this side of eternity.

On the other hand, there are some divisions within the visible church that are frivolous and avoidable—as Paul addresses in 1 Corinthians 1:12–13. Different people wrongly divided along the lines of earthly leaders in the early church such as Paul, Apollos, or Cephas. In the same way, modern congregations and members of churches are tempted to do the same. Some local congregations divide over the color of the carpeting in the sanctuary. Some individuals may leave because of a personality clash with another member of the congregation.

9. **How can our fellowship as the Body of Christ be a sign to unbelievers? According to Matthew 5:14–16, what has God called the church to do? How do frivolous and avoidable divisions in the church hurt our witness to the world?**

Reflecting the undivided harmony of the invisible church, the visible church is ever and always aimed at unity and fellowship. By the power of the Holy Spirit, doctrinal unity leads to fellowship as the Body of Christ for all the world to see. Our fellowship as the Body of Christ is a sign to the world—and especially to unbelievers—that we follow Christ Jesus. Instead of seeing a mess of people following a mess of worldly leaders and opinions, the world should see the visible church following Jesus.

We live in a world marked by disunity and dissension. As such, we are tempted to think that convictions cause people to disagree and that having fewer and weaker convictions will result in more and greater agreement. In reality, however, what we believe, teach, and confess promotes true and meaningful fellowship. Reflecting the will of God, the Holy Spirit is at work in and through the doctrinal deliberations of the visible church as we strive to live in unity and harmony with one another. We exercise humility, gentleness, patience, and love for one another as we sort through minor and major divisions. As united followers of Jesus, the Body of Christ shines the light of Jesus for all the world to see.

Do we go to church primarily to get something out of it?

Mac or PC? Android or Apple? Nike or Adidas? Ford or GM?

The answers that you give to these questions distinguish you from others; the ways that you respond to these questions may differ from your family and friends. However, no matter how your answers may differ from someone else, they all place a common label on you: consumer.

The world of commerce sees people as consumers. The world tells us that we consume to live and we live to consume. Advertisements make it appear as if our entire identity is established by the brands we wear, the gadgets we own, and the foods we eat. As such, it is very easy to transfer the logic of the marketplace to the church. This can result in a misconception about the church and what happens as we gather for worship—that we are consumers coming to church to get something out of it. We become church shoppers.

The church does not conform to the logic of the marketplace. Instead, God has something bigger—and better—in mind for us as we go to church and gather together for the Divine Service.

1. **Read John 4:7–15. What does Jesus promise (vv. 13–14) to the Samaritan woman at the well? Is the woman expecting something earthly and physical or something spiritual and eternal? How might we develop proper expectations for what we receive from the church and worship?**

The interchange between this Samaritan woman and Jesus helps us identify some important questions that we should ask about the church and worship: What benefit do we receive from church? Do I come to church only to receive?

In one sense, we should come to church expecting to receive. In the Divine Service, we receive a superabundance of the means of grace. Just as Jesus used water to describe God's gift of living water, we can think of God's grace as being like a waterfall. Imagine standing underneath a waterfall as thousands and thousands of gallons of water descend down from above (see James 1:17). This is what it is like to receive God's grace in the Divine Service. Like standing under a waterfall with open hands, we gather in the Divine Service with open hands to receive God's grace in Christ Jesus. The grace of God that has come down from heaven in Jesus comes to us in the means of grace, which God delivers in worship.

2. What are some of the means of grace we receive with open hands in the Divine Service?

So, it is not entirely wrong to come to church with the expectation of receiving. We come to church and the Divine Service to receive the means of grace, which God gives in worship. Yet we do not receive these gifts according to the logic of the marketplace or commerce. Unlike consumer products, we do not purchase the means of grace with our money or our efforts. God does not pay out forgiveness because we pour our heart and soul into the songs that we sing in worship. Nor does God meet us halfway by giving us His grace only after we have adequately tried our best to be holy. Rather, God pours out the means of grace in worship apart from our efforts and merits. The price has been paid through the cross and resurrection of Jesus—through faith, we simply receive with open hands!

3. **Read Romans 12:1–8. According to these verses, do we come to church only to receive? What are we to do with the grace that we receive in Christ Jesus? How does living worship flow out of the means of grace that we receive in the Divine Service?**

Like water flowing through our hands, the means of grace and the gifts of God that we receive in worship flow from God to us and from us to the world.

How can you serve others as part of the church? First and foremost, you serve others by proclaiming the Good News of Christ Jesus. The Word of God that you hear and receive in worship is not meant to be bottled inside of you; God's Word and Gospel promises are meant to be shared with others in need of the hope of Jesus.

4. **Read Romans 12:6–8. How else are we to use the gifts that God pours out on us?**

We come to church to receive. And having gathered for the Divine Service, where we receive a divine flood of grace, we direct the flow of God's gifts toward our neighbors. Being part of the church is not for silos but for sieves. We do not silo God's gifts only for ourselves. Instead, we are like a sieve with God's grace and gifts as they flow in loving service to our neighbors.

As we have already discussed, the church is a mysteriously beautiful gift of God. Though God uses human hands and voices, efforts and endeavors within the church on earth, it is His church and the Body of Christ. One of the ways that God empowers the church is by the person and work of the Holy Spirit.

5. Read Acts 2:1–4, 42–47. How was the work of the Holy Spirit evident in the early church?

Though these special outpourings of the Holy Spirit were confined to the apostolic period of the early church, this does not mean that the Holy Spirit is not still present and active in the church today.

6. How does the Holy Spirit empower the church to support one another today? Look especially at Acts 2:42, 46.

Just as it was in the early church, the Holy Spirit calls people by the Gospel, enlightens us with His gifts, sanctifies and keeps us in the true faith. The Holy Spirit adds day by day those who are being saved.

Yet similar to God's work in the church in other ways, the Holy Spirit uses our human hands and voices, efforts and endeavors. When you give to brothers and sisters in need, the Holy Spirit is working through you to support the Body of Christ. When you break bread and pray with others, the Holy Spirit is using you to strengthen and encourage the church. When you gather for worship and use your time, talents, and treasures to serve your neighbors, the Holy Spirit is looming behind you in a powerful way. Now that you have received the Holy Spirit, God uses you as a vessel of the Holy Spirit for the life of the world!

We have explored many different misconceptions and questions about the church. And yet there are many misconceptions and questions about the church that still remain. This should come as no surprise: this seemingly ordinary thing that we call church is a mysteriously beautiful gift of God. Veiled by human hands and voices, efforts and endeavors, God is at work finding, gathering, and forgiving sinners in and through the church. The next time you gather together at church for worship or fellowship, take a moment to marvel at the extraordinary work of the Father, Son, and Holy Spirit that happens in this place.

Closing Prayer

> *Lord God, I marvel at the extraordinary work that You do through the church. Let me never see the church as just an ordinary place made by human hands, but instead, let me see it as You see it: the extraordinary place where Your grace in Christ Jesus is poured out to overflowing. In Jesus' name. Amen.*

ABOUT THE SACRAMENTS

MISCONCEPTIONS ABOUT THE SACRAMENTS

- **We can't trust that Baptism will save us.**
- **Unbaptized adults don't need to receive Baptism; a person can be saved just as well without it.**
- **If we take Communion too often, it will become less meaningful for us.**

Opening Prayer

Heavenly Father, let me see Your sacramental gifts as a blessing in my life. May I continually return to the renewing grace found within them. Grant me the knowledge of the fullness of the assurance found in my Baptism and the confidence of Your mercy found in Your Supper. In Jesus' name. Amen.

Introduction

In the life of the church, the Sacraments play a key role. Baptism and the Lord's Supper are gifts from God for the life of the Christian. Through physical means, God delivers His promises for His people. God does not need them; His people do. In this, we see the words of James 1:17 vividly displayed: "Every good gift and every perfect gift is from above, coming down from the Father of lights, with whom there is no variation or shadow due to change." These Sacraments are not required, rote religious rites. Instead, they are the active gifts God gives His people.

Yet they are mysterious. Simple water, bread, and wine are powerfully intertwined with the Word of God to provide assurance and forgiveness. Can we trust these everyday, ordinary things to convey the promises of God to us?

Can I trust that since I'm baptized, I'm saved?

Baptism is a simple thing—water plus the Word of God combined to deliver the promises of God, salvation through bathing. John the Baptist received his moniker because he was going around baptizing people. It was not a new idea at the time of Jesus. Yet it takes on new significance when Jesus enters the Jordan, John declaring he is not worthy to baptize Him. Something different happens. Baptism becomes more than a symbolic washing of sins and instead is now connected directly to the work of the Savior. It becomes active and real, not role play.

1. **Do you know your baptismal birthday? If so, do you do anything to celebrate it? What do you do?**

But how do we trust that this act can save us? Baptism is just water and words, so how could it possibly convey the assurance of salvation?

First, can water really do this? The foundational belief in the work of the Sacraments is grounded in the fact that God uses physical things to deliver salvation. It might be hard to think that God could use these simple items to bring about the amazing works promised in the Sacraments. If we ask, "Can I trust my Baptism saves me?" we must first wonder if water could convey that salvation to us. God's grace and mercy are often delivered to His people via physical means.

2. **Let's look at an example from Scripture. God was going to deliver His people from Egypt. Moses was the one God chose to take on this task. Read Exodus 4:1–5; 7:10–13, 20; 14:16. How did God use physical means to reassure Moses and display His power? What wonders did He work through Moses and Aaron using that physical means?**

The cinematic imagination would say God imbued power into this wooden stick. In this line of thinking, one day, an Indiana Jones–type archaeologist would discover the magical instrument and use it to unleash power and might unseen since the plagues. But that is not the case. God uses this staff not because He needs it but because His people do. In it, they can look and see that God's might is on their side. But should Moses try to use it for his own gain, it will simply be a stick. It is the created element combined with the power, might, and will of God. The staff does not work the miracles; instead, God displays His power through it.

3. **Take a moment to brainstorm the following: What are some other physical things God has used, both in the Old and New Testaments, to bring justice, mercy, and hope to His people?**

Looking through the places God has brought hope to His people through physical things reveals a pattern throughout Scripture. God works through created things. He uses them for the sake of His people. Now we can answer this question: Can water really do this? If it were just water, the answer would be no.

But Baptism is not water on its own. Instead, it is water coupled with the Spirit of God and His Word to accomplish what He intends it to do.

The water is not holy. While it is an incredible blessing to baptize in church buildings with a font that has seen generations of sinners transformed to saints, we know that those things are not necessary. The Ethiopian eunuch knew this when he looked at Philip and said, "See, here is water! What prevents me from being baptized?" (Acts 8:36). Water and the Word is all you need. Water does this thing not because of the pipes it runs through or what basin it may rest in at the time of Baptism. No, it is a physical means created by God that He uses to bless His people. It is not a ritual performed for God. Water is used for our benefit. It is a gift that God gives so that our assurance of salvation is anchored to what He has done. The water is not symbolic of God's work; it *is* God's work.

But it cannot be water alone. The water, whether a puddle or a crystal-clear spring, becomes something altogether new when used in conjunction with the Word of God. His Spirit uses this water to do what He says it will.

4. Let's look more at the connection between the Holy Spirit, the Word, and water. Read these Scripture passages and discuss what they reveal about that connection in Baptism.

- **Matthew 3:11:**
- **John 3:3–6:**

Baptism is now more than just water. In it, God attaches Himself to a simple, created thing for the benefit of His people. Baptism is water, Word, and Spirit all together brought in power to deliver to God's people the salvation that Christ won for them in His death and resurrection.

God uses physical means to accomplish His work. He uses elements in the world He created to deliver His grace and mercy for the benefit of His people.

But why do we even need this? What is the point of Baptism?

5. **Read Titus 3:3–7. Then, breaking down the points in those verses, answer the following questions.**

- **Why do we need a Savior?**

- **How does God provide for us in our need?**

- **What does this passage tell us we receive in Baptism?**

The Scriptures declare this to us. We are a people in need. Sin has destroyed us. Yet God in His infinite mercy brought salvation to us through His Son. Even as people who have become saints through Baptism, we still struggle with the sin we inherited at birth. Throughout the Bible, God's people see His miraculous work but still turn away from Him.

6. **Consider the Israelites after God freed them from Egypt. Read Exodus 14:10–12; 32:1–4. What caused the Israelites to turn from God in these accounts?**

7. **It might be easy to think this only happened to those people before Jesus came down to earth. But consider Peter. He walked with Jesus through His earthly ministry. He was present as Jesus made the lame to walk, healed lepers, turned water to wine, and called Lazarus out of the tomb. Yet what did Peter do in Luke 22:56–61?**

The Israelites turned from God again and again. Peter, an apostle, denied Jesus three times even after seeing the power of the kingdom of God. God understands that His people are fickle and foolish. Our eyes will be drawn to things we think will fulfill us. When those things fail us, we begin to question what we know. Peter would weep over his denial. The people of Israel lived in a cycle of wandering and lamenting. Robert Robinson captured this reality in the hymn "Come, Thou Fount of Every Blessing" with this beautiful line: "Prone to wander, Lord, I feel it; Prone to leave the God I love" (*LSB* 686:3). We want to remain, but we are prone to wander, prone to leave.

8. **In Baptism, God provides an anchor. Read the following passages and consider the comfort and assurance of these promises from our God.**

- **John 3:5:**
- **Romans 6:4:**
- **1 Peter 3:21:**

The devil whispers the lie in our ears: "Could you possibly be saved? You are a broken sinner!" But our Baptism declares victory over those falsehoods! As saints struggling with sin, we are still prone to wander, but our Baptism has sealed our place in the kingdom of God! It is trustworthy and true that when asked "Are you a Christian?" all we need answer is "I was baptized!" Baptism is the beginning of the journey of the life of a follower of Jesus. In that, our salvation is secure.

This mysterious work of water, Word, and Spirit takes God's grace and binds it, without release, to us. Can we trust that if we are baptized, we are saved? Yes! Because it is not our work. It is the way in which God has always worked—combining the physical world with His spiritual power to deliver mercy to His people. We don't get baptized to "prove" we believe in the redemptive work of Jesus. In our Baptism, God delivers His redemptive work to us. We do not choose Him; He has chosen us.

Do unbaptized adults need to receive Baptism? Can't a person be saved just as well without it?

Baptism is a Sacrament—that is, God delivering His grace through a physical means. While God may bring mercy and justice through other natural ways, only Baptism and the Lord's Supper deliver the grace He promised. Thus, they are the only two Sacraments. As Baptism works as a gift for the assurance and action of salvation, it is a blessing to God's people.

Now, there is a classic question about Baptism. Hypothetically, if a person hears the Good News of Jesus and is walking across the street to be baptized, is struck by a bus, and dies, is he or she saved? The quick answer is yes. But the tension remains. If Baptism wasn't "necessary" for that person to be saved, then why even bother? Breaking down this question will benefit our walk in faith.

To break down this question, let's turn to the account of Philip and the Ethiopian eunuch. This account is of great relevance to the discussion of Baptism and how it works in daily life. The question of baptizing adults versus children, the importance of Baptism, and the argument that Baptism is unnecessary for salvation all have an answer, or a start to an answer, within these verses.

1. **Read the Ethiopian eunuch's story in Acts 8:26–34. What details stand out to you?**

2. **Now read Matthew 18:3–4. Considering the reading from Acts and this passage from Matthew, what is different about the faith of children and the way adults come to faith? Why do we baptize children with little to no knowledge of the faith but have adults go through a process of learning first? Do children remain with no knowledge of the faith?**

Does Baptism need lifelong learning as a disciple following Jesus? Yes. Does not possessing that knowledge invalidate Baptism? No. Baptism conveys childlike faith—that which trusts when there is no reason to trust.

Thus, for adults coming to faith, there is a reverse learning curve. Children come to faith and then grow up in the knowledge of who God is, but adults will need to learn and see how God interacts with this fallen world.

3. Read the following passages. How do these verses relate to this idea?

- **Romans 6:3–5:**

- **Proverbs 3:5:**

But is Baptism even important?

Let's start to answer this by returning to the story of the Ethiopian eunuch. As Philip tells the man what Isaiah is talking about in his prophecies, the Holy Spirit is at work. Asking questions, delving deeper, the eunuch is being prompted to discover more about who Jesus is. Philip continues to share the Good News. Notice what happens in verse 36: "And as they were going along the road they came to some water, and the eunuch said, 'See, here is water! What prevents me from being baptized?'"

Descriptors for the type of water are limited. Was it a watering hole for local livestock? a flowing stream? a puddle? We do not know. But what we do know is that after hearing the Good News of Jesus, the eunuch has one question: "What prevents me from being baptized?" It is not about him making a decision to forgo his old life or a rote prayer to declare his allegiance to a new faith. No. He asks a simple question: "What prevents me from being baptized?"

God's prompting in the heart of the eunuch worked through the physical world: the scroll of Isaiah, the person of Philip, then simple water. Each of these held significance in guiding him toward faith. If it had been only the words of Isaiah, would the Ethiopian man have not stopped there with his own understanding? What about if it had simply been Philip's explanation and telling the story of Jesus? But instead, the man is prompted toward Baptism. Through his short time in speaking with Philip, he understood that Baptism is the logical next step. The importance of Baptism cannot be understated.

4. **Read the passages below. How do they emphasize the importance of Baptism?**

- **Matthew 28:19:**

- **Ephesians 4:4–6:**

5. **This leads us to one of the biggest questions about Baptism as a Sacrament from God: Is Baptism necessary to be saved? Consider the importance the Ethiopian man placed on it, immediately asking to be baptized after talking to Philip. Read the following passages from the book of Acts. What is the common response in all of them?**

- **Acts 2:38:**
- **Acts 8:12:**
- **Acts 10:47–48:**
- **Acts 16:14–15:**
- **Acts 16:30–33:**
- **Acts 19:5:**
- **Acts 22:16:**

Whenever someone hears the Good News of Jesus, they move to be baptized. Baptism is necessary to be saved. When the Holy Spirit moves the Gospel to take root, Baptism is always present.

The Apology to the Augsburg Confession responds clearly to the misconception that Baptism is not necessary to be saved: "We confess that 'Baptism is necessary for salvation,' that 'children are to be baptized,' and that the 'Baptism of children is not in vain, but is necessary and effective for salvation'" (Article IX 51).

Baptism is necessary because that's how God wills it to be. It is a gift that allows us to have a firm foundation in His assurance, not our own will. The passages above from the book of Acts show us that belief and Baptism are not separate but completely connected. Whole households were baptized in the book of Acts. We can assume this includes children of all ages. Adult converts rushed to Baptism because they saw it as the first step of life in Jesus. Salvation is given through Baptism for our benefit. It is a gift of God for us, a gift upon a gift.

That brings us back to the question of the person who is struck by the bus on the way to Baptism. Will they be saved? The answer is yes. The reason Baptism saves us is not the water. It's not even saying the right words. It is because that water, those words, are backed up by Jesus. Jesus looked at the thief on the cross and said, "Truly, I say to you, today you will be with Me in paradise" (Luke 23:43). The work was not the thief's; it was Jesus' declaration and work that He accomplished on the cross. It is not muttering the right thing; it is that the Savior of the world backs up those words. So, too, in Baptism, Jesus backs up the water and the Word. He is the one who brings the Baptism of rebirth and fire, as John testified (see Matthew 3:11). The Holy Spirit is ushered into all Christians because of the cross and empty tomb. Then, Jesus is the one who declares righteousness. We can trust the words that Baptism now saves.

How often should we commune? If we do it too often, won't it become less meaningful for us?

Jesus does a peculiar thing during Holy Week. While gathered with His disciples in the Upper Room, He takes the Jewish Passover meal and makes it into something more. Sitting with those who have been following Him most closely, He looks to them as He breaks bread and says, "This is My body." Then as the cup of wine is prepared to be passed around, He says, "This is My blood." He states that both are given for the forgiveness of sins. Just as God had passed over the houses of the Israelites smeared with blood during the exodus from Egypt, now God's judgment passes over those who have partaken in the meal of the body and blood of the Messiah.

Again God works through simple means to deliver His grace. It's a meal instituted not for God but for His people. In this meal, Jesus meets His people wherever they are gathered to bring assurance and forgiveness in a way that can be seen and touched. It is a physical gift for people struggling as they live in a real world.

1. **When did you first receive Communion? Do you remember how you felt at the time? How often do you receive Communion now?**

....

....

....

....

Why is this meal important for Christians?

Think about the last time you did a hard workout. Sweating and breathing heavy, you took a drink from a cool glass of water. You can feel that water at work—the hydration moves through your system, renewing you to keep going.

Taking Communion is like this but for the life of a Christian. It is a renewal of the covenant promises that God gives His people. But this meal is not a physical refreshing. In the Lord's Supper, weary travelers find rest, broken souls are mended, and the Body of Christ rejoices together in the work of Jesus for them. This meal is a renewal given by God to Christians as they walk in a fallen world. When the question sneaks into the minds of the followers of Jesus, "Could I possibly be forgiven?" the Lord's Supper declares that they have been forgiven. As the enemy whispers lies of defeat and dread, this meal drowns them out by blessing those who partake with grace upon grace.

Communion is a celebration, healing balm, and time machine all wrapped into one. This meal proclaims a celebration of Jesus' work on the cross and through the empty tomb. A Savior came and did the work God promised He would do. Through the body and blood of Christ, healing is given. These elements bring what Jesus says they would, namely, forgiveness. It's not simply a nice reminder that we are forgiven, but in a beautiful mystery, the elements are given for God's people to experience and receive the blessings of the Gospel in a tangible way.

An unexplainable thing happens in the midst of this meal. Space and time are warped around the bread and wine. While partaking of the Lamb's feast, the participant is brought together with all the saints—those who have gone before, those who are standing with him or her, and those who are to come. This meal unites the church in a real way. Here it is that the Savior meets us and here it is that He gives us a glimpse of what the true unity we have as His believers will look like in the new heaven and new earth.

All of these benefits work together for us. Simple bread, simple wine becoming the vehicles for the blessings of the Creator of the universe. This is important. A wise elder of a church was once a broken record reminding his pastor, "We don't call it a worship service because we are here to serve God. We call it that because He is here to serve us." We are not like devotees of a pagan god, showing up to provide sacrifice and ritual for a craven image of wood and stone. Instead, our God breaks the mold and steps down to deliver His kingdom to us. This is a cornerstone of the Christian life.

2. **Let's look at how Paul talks about this meal. Read 1 Corinthians 10:16–17. What promises of God does Paul say come through Communion?**

God not only delivers on His promise, but He does it again and again in a way that His people can touch, taste, and see. While we await Christ's return as saints still struggling in a world of sin, this meal is a deliverance to our troubled consciences.

Is Communion more about our experience or about what God is doing for us? The answer to this question is a resounding yes! Rather than two opposing ideas, our experience and God's work are bound together as we partake in the meal. Our moods and experiences may shift, as they often do, but God's work is always steadfast. Yet the two are interwoven. The work of God will always mean this meal will be an experience in our lives.

Whether it feels ordinary or mysteriously supernatural, the Lord's Supper is still effective because Jesus is the one doing the action. God created humans with both logic and emotion. There will be days when partaking in the Lord's Supper will bring about a rush of emotion as we realize the depth of love God displays for us through this gift. There will also be times when our experience will lean heavily on the truth and knowledge of what God is doing, because our sensation of the meal does not reflect the reality. But on both of those days, the meal still delivers what God has promised. His promise means that while our experience may change, His gift never does.

3. **Read John 6:47–56. What reality does Jesus promise comes by this meal? How does this comfort us when we don't particularly "feel" God when we take Communion? How does this ground us and explain the depth of our feelings when we do have a more emotional experience with Communion?**

No matter how we feel when we take Communion, God's promise to abide in us through this meal has not waned.

So how often should we commune? And will taking Communion more often make it less meaningful for us?

4. **Read Acts 2:42. How does this short verse describing the practices of the early church speak to these questions?**

Part of the early church's gathering together included this meal. All throughout the New Testament as the church forms, the Lord's Supper is a cornerstone of their life together.

There is no exact formula for how often Communion should be taken. The best response is to take it as often as your church offers the opportunity to come together around the body and blood! Remember, Communion is not a religious rite we are doing for God. It is not a way for us to please Him. Instead, He brings this meal for us. Because of this, we should partake as often as our church takes the meal and we are able. But also remember that this is a family meal. It is not meant to be taken alone as a personal devotion; it is for the saints gathered together, as the Acts passage illustrates.

Taking Communion regularly will not lessen its impact. We are constantly struggling with sin. The Lord's Supper is not for perfect people. It is a meal given for those in need of forgiveness. In the Lord's Supper, we find the declaration that sin does not rule us anymore, and the gift of deliverance and forgiveness from God. It renews us for a life lived as the people of God.

As he sees Jesus, John the Baptist proclaims, "Behold, the Lamb of God, who takes away the sin of the world!" (John 1:29). As we come together for Communion, we, too, see Jesus through His body and blood and can proclaim the Savior who has taken our sin. Then, partaking together, we experience that beautiful mystery of the Messiah coming to serve us through this meal.

Closing Prayer

Lord, may we rejoice that You would give us the Sacraments. You have blessed us with the assurance that they provide. May we constantly be reminded of the waters of our Baptism, when You brought us into Your kingdom. Let those waters be a balm to us as a blessing of confidence in our salvation. Thank You for the gift of Your meal, which delivers forgiveness to us throughout our lives following You. Forgiveness and mercy follow us all our lives through these gifts. In Jesus' name we pray. Amen.

ABOUT WORSHIP AND PRAYER

MISCONCEPTIONS ABOUT WORSHIP AND PRAYER

- **Prayer changes things.**
- **Having a good personal prayer life is more important than meaningful corporate worship.**
- **If I don't get anything out of liturgical worship, I should find another way to worship.**

Opening Prayer

Almighty God, send upon us Your Spirit so that we might be moved to bring all our cares and concerns to You and trust and accept Your holy will in our lives. Through Jesus Christ our Lord. Amen.

Introduction

Hardly anything is more central to the Christian life than worship and prayer. In fact, if you ask a stranger on the street or a random acquaintance online what it means to be a Christian, he or she will probably say something like, "Well, Christians go to church, they pray to God, and they try to be good people." But because these notions are so commonplace in our world, they're also accompanied by a lot of misunderstandings. Often, people's *perception* of what a Christian is, or how to worship, or what it means to pray are filtered through their own personal and cultural experiences rather than God's Word. Even among Christians, our notions about these central religious activities can sometimes become skewed toward self or society rather than what the Lord would teach us.

In this session, we'll clear up some of those misconceptions and tackle some of the big questions about worship and prayer. Sometimes our notions will have partial truth in them but might need clarification or refocus based upon Scripture. Also, remember that no aspect of the Christian life will ever achieve perfection on this side of eternity—including our own thoughts about God! Finally, be patient with yourself and with others as we wrestle with the big issues. In this world, "we see in a mirror dimly," as Paul put it (1 Corinthians 13:12). There will never be a time without mystery as we contemplate the things of God. Sometimes we just need to embrace the mystery and trust that our loving Father will walk with us through whatever big questions we might have.

Does prayer change things?

1. **Think about times in your life when you prayed fervently to the Lord for something. Perhaps it was a specific act of healing, a prayer for guidance through a difficult time, a prayer for discernment about a particular issue. If you feel comfortable, share one instance when your prayer was answered as you had hoped and another when it wasn't.**

Perhaps the best place to start in understanding prayer is to turn to Jesus Himself. The Gospels are full of examples of the fully human Jesus turning to His heavenly Father in prayer.

2. **Read the account in Matthew 26:36–46 of Jesus' prayer in the Garden of Gethsemane. How does Jesus conclude His heartfelt prayer? Why might this model be the most difficult yet the most important feature of Christian prayer?**

Trust is at the center of Jesus' model of prayer. If we know that the heart of God is love for us, we know that whatever His answer to our prayer might be, it is for our benefit. We also can be confident that He will walk with us, no matter how difficult the road that lies ahead.

In the final moments before His betrayal, our Lord spent time in prayer specifically for us. How inspiring to know that we, His followers, were on His mind before the horrific events of His trial, suffering, and death on the cross!

3. **Read Jesus' prayer for us from John 17:20–25. If you knew that your own death might come in a matter of hours, what might your final prayer be like? What did Jesus pray for? What was the purpose of His request (v. 21)?**

Jesus prayed that God would change *us*. Likewise, when we pray, we ask the Lord to reshape our hearts and wills to be unified with Him and with our Christian brothers and sisters in the work of the Gospel.

4. **With darkness overshadowing the land, and the sins of the whole world upon Him, Jesus cried out to God, quoting Psalm 22:1, "My God, My God, why have You forsaken Me?" Read Matthew 27:45–50, the account of Christ's death on the cross. Have you ever allowed yourself to ask God "Why?" Did you feel a tinge of guilt for uttering such a prayer? How might Jesus' example give us permission to be honest with God in our most difficult moments? What other examples can you think of in Scripture when people brought their tough questions and emotions to God in prayer?**

Of course, the Almighty already knows how we feel, but it's comforting to know that He's strong enough and loving enough to take whatever we might throw at Him. We might not stay in a prayer of lament, but we can certainly start there. Many of our most difficult "Why?" prayers will remain unanswered on this side of eternity. However, knowing that Christ's love for us at the cross is stronger than anything helps us ask the toughest questions and pray the most difficult prayers while still walking forward in faith.

5. **Read the following examples from Paul regarding prayer. What do you note regarding both the who and the what of his prayers?**

- **1 Corinthians 1:4–9:**
- **Ephesians 1:15–17:**
- **Philippians 1:3–6:**
- **Romans 1:8–10:**

The apostle Paul prays constantly and fervently for others—in thanksgiving for their partnership in the Gospel and in the hope that their faith in Christ would grow. While we should always be mindful of the physical and earthly needs of others, our priority in prayer remains spiritual.

6. **Other than in church or at home, share some specific places where you've prayed. What's one of the stranger settings in which you've talked to God? The prophet Jonah prayed in a strange place—from within the belly of a great fish! Read his prayer in Jonah 2. What are some things that jump out at you about his prayer? To whom is the prayer specifically addressed?**

Jonah's cries ascended to the One he knew would hear him and who could actually do something about his situation. Jonah specifically dismissed clinging to worthless idols who have no power and instead clearly confessed, "Salvation belongs to the LORD!" (Jonah 2:9).

7. **Does God promise to give us whatever we pray for "in Jesus' name"? Read John 14:13–14 and 1 John 5:13–15. Often, Christians misunderstand the phrase "in Jesus' name" to function like a magic incantation or secret password that, when stuck at the end of a prayer, guarantees its success. How does the context surrounding these passages help clarify what Jesus means by "in My name"?**

By our Baptism "in Jesus' name," we can be assured of the constant flow of forgiveness for the many times our prayers, our deeds, and our intentions fall short of the glory of His name. How good to know Christ's grace for His frail and imperfect children! Because we have been baptized into His name, we also know that the Holy Spirit, whom Jesus constantly pours out upon His church through the Word and Sacraments, works within us, sanctifying both our work and our prayers.

When King Solomon completed the temple for God's people in Jerusalem, some hailed it as one of the most impressive houses of worship ever built. Indeed, the king expended vast amounts of treasure and manpower constructing a house worthy of God's presence. Yet when completed, Solomon began his prayer of dedication acknowledging the inadequacy of all his efforts.

8. **Read the start of Solomon's prayer in 1 Kings 8:22–30. What might this honest and humble prayer of Solomon tell us about our own efforts in worship and prayer? In what ways might Solomon's prayer help remodel your own?**

We can't put the Lord into even the best of earthly temples, just like we can't put Him in a box. We can't confine Him, cajole Him, or corner Him into giving us what we want. Not even the great temple of Solomon was big enough or beautiful enough to contain the maker of heaven and earth. And yet our loving and gracious Lord, for our sake, bids us to call upon Him in prayer and provides places of worship for us. But this is because *we* need it, and not because *He* needs it.

9. **Read again 1 Kings 8:27–30. Why might it be significant that God said of the temple, "My name shall be there" (1 Kings 8:29)? That is, since God placed His name upon the temple, what assurance might that give to the worshipers? What comfort and assurance might this also give to your prayers "in Jesus' name"?**

Christians recognize the name of Jesus as "the name that is above every name" (Philippians 2:9) and that "there is no other name under heaven given among men by which we must be saved" (Acts 4:12). As God placed His name and therefore His promise upon the temple in the Old Testament, now in Christ, He has done so again—only now, this promise is for all people.

10. **Read further in Solomon's prayer. In 1 Kings 8:27–53, how many times does the king repeat a form of the phrase "hear and forgive"? We know that because of the work of Christ Jesus on the cross for us, our sins have been forgiven and we are made God's beloved sons and daughters. How might the knowledge of this Gospel message embolden our prayer life?**

Solomon's prayer of dedication can be outlined by its themes. For example, he offers a prayer of vindication (seeking God's justice), of repentance (turning from sin), of relief (help in times of distress), of mission (God's call to all nations), of victory (seeking defeat over enemies), and of compassion (God looking upon us in mercy).

11. **If you were to outline the themes of your own prayers, what might they be? What do you think should be the themes of a mature Christian's prayers?**

So, does the Bible give us specific instructions regarding prayer?

The answer is yes! When Jesus taught His disciples what we now call the Lord's Prayer, He reminded them that their heavenly Father already knew their needs before they even began to pray. Yet Jesus still gave them the words to say.

12. **Read the Lord's Prayer as it is recorded in Matthew 6:5–13. How is the wording perhaps slightly different than what we're used to? While we pray the specific words of the Lord's Prayer, it can also function as an outline for how we pray and what kind of things we should ask for. Discuss the themes outlined in Jesus' words. (Luther's teaching on the Lord's Prayer in the Small Catechism might be helpful in this regard.)**

....

....

....

It's noteworthy that only one petition—the fourth, on "daily bread"—specifically asks for material help. This insight helps guide the content of our prayers, steering them away from simple "gimme" requests and toward the more mature petitions asking for joyfulness, thankfulness, and contentment in whatever God gives us.

13. **Read Romans 8:22–27, where Paul comforts the Roman Christians with the knowledge that, even when we can't pray, the Holy Spirit prays for us. Can you think of a time when you just couldn't find the words to say? Or perhaps, in exhaustion, you could no longer muster the energy for prayer? What might the content of the Spirit's "groanings" be for us?**

....

....

....

Baptized Christians have been given the Holy Spirit and are renewed and strengthened in their faith through the means of grace. The Bible provides many forms and words for prayer, which can be helpful when we don't know how to pray. The Psalms—sometimes called the prayer book of the Bible—are a great example. The hymns and liturgies of the church—drawn from the Scriptures and thousands of years of Christian experience—are another great resource. Simply reading a hymn text out loud can be an effective form of prayer.

However, we also know that prayer is beyond words. It is deeper than articulation and understanding. How comforting to know that with the gift of the Holy Spirit comes an unceasing, perfect prayer to the Father on our behalf!

In every case of answered prayer in Scripture, the prayer itself had no power to change anything. Rather, it was the Lord hearing the petition who, out of goodness and mercy for His people, responded with not exactly what they wanted but what His will was for them. We might say that prayer changes *us*. That is, through prayer, our wills are bent toward the will of God, not the other way around.

We're urged in the Scriptures to "pray without ceasing" (1 Thessalonians 5:17). Jesus reminds us to be persistent always in prayer (Luke 18:1–8). But at the heart of all of our prayers is trust in God's good and gracious will for us. As Paul put it, "He who did not spare His own Son but gave Him up for us all, how will He not also with Him graciously give us all things?" (Romans 8:32). This trust in Christ's love and faithfulness knows that we won't always get what we want when we want it, but that whatever we receive, we receive from the hand of a gracious God.

Jesus Himself uses the analogy of a loving parent (see Matthew 7:7–11) to help us understand prayer. A good and caring parent loves to hear from his or her children, even if the parent already knows what the children need. This helps us understand that prayer is ultimately more about relationship than results. God, our heavenly Father, is infinitely stronger, wiser, and more loving than the best earthly parent. How much more, then, should we continually turn to Him in prayer and trust both His timing and His will for our lives?

Is having a good personal prayer life more important than meaningful corporate worship?

Individual expressions of piety as well as corporate worship are both important and, indeed, encouraged throughout the Scriptures. Jesus Himself might be the best example, as our Lord often went off by Himself to pray but also regularly worshiped with His fellow Jews and His closest disciples.

Our contemporary world is becoming more and more fragmented and individualistic, however, and this poses a real danger to us and the church. In some ways, through online media and the breadth and scope of the internet, we are more connected with more people than ever before. At the same time, loneliness, depression, and anxiety have risen to unprecedented levels. Our deep loneliness and longing for true community is masked by a pervasive but shallow "connectedness." Our study of God's Word will help us appreciate the Christian community we have, encourage deeper and more lasting ties with one another, and caution against separating ourselves further from the Body of Christ.

1. **"I don't get anything out of it." "I can worship God just as well on my own." "My life is busy enough. I don't need one more thing to do on a weekend." "Those people at the church hurt my feelings years ago." "It's really hard getting everyone up and out of the house on a Sunday morning." These are just some of the reasons people might list in avoiding going to church for public worship. Think of other excuses you may have heard. What are some of the most legitimate reasons? What are some of the worst excuses you've heard?**

....

....

....

2. **Now read Hebrews 10:19–25. The writer of the book of Hebrews urges public worship along with holding to the Gospel and spurring one another on to love and good works. Why do you think he mentions the "Day drawing near" at the end of verse 25? How might that give urgency to the command to worship together?**

....

....

....

While there are, of course, many understandable and legitimate reasons people cannot worship with the Body of Christ—people who are homebound, hospitalized, or otherwise incapacitated, for example—the default for the Christian should be worshiping *together.*

God has affixed many blessings to His command to worship together. Some of them might not seem to be blessings at first glance. For example, by gathering with other people and being part of a Christian community, I am sometimes painfully reminded of my own faults as well as the faults of others.

3. **How might isolating ourselves from others inhibit our growth as Christians? What gifts of the Holy Spirit might be needed to keep a Christian community together?**

4. **Sometimes we get stuck on the question "What can I get out of worshiping with others?" But let's turn that question around. What answers might surface if we instead ask, "What can I give in worshiping with others?"**

Jesus regularly participated in the public festivals and worship life of God's people. In fact, on several important occasions, He used the temple or synagogue worship as an opportunity to proclaim God's kingdom fulfilled in His own person and work.

5. **Read Luke 4:14–21 and John 7:37–38. What does the Lord's example tell us about the importance of being together in worship?**

6. **Read Matthew 26:26–30. As Jesus shares the Passover with His disciples, He also knows all that will unfold for Him in the next few hours. How might singing with His brothers have brought Him encouragement? Share with one another some of your favorite hymns or Christian songs and why they're important to you.**

Jesus sang praises and read God's Word with His closest friends to prepare Him for His darkest hour. It's likely they would have sung Psalms 115–118 together to conclude the Passover meal. Their voices, joined with His, filled the Upper Room with the praises and promises of God.

7. **Read Psalm 117. How might the words of this hymn have challenged and encouraged the disciples in a difficult time?**

The early church provides more examples for us of the benefits of following God's command to worship together. On the day of Pentecost, the book of Acts says that the first disciples were "all together in one place" (2:1) when the Holy Spirit rushed upon them and used them to proclaim Christ to people of "every nation under heaven" (2:5). In a way, our time of worship together in God's house functions like a reenactment of that first Pentecost: people from all different backgrounds and nations together in one place, filled with the Spirit, proclaiming in word and song the wonders of God. We can certainly hear and celebrate the Gospel individually, but how much more joyful is the celebration when we join together with the fellow redeemed!

8. **Read Acts 2:42–47. These six verses can be summed up in one word: community. Outline the different features of this Christian community. Which do you find most appealing? Why?**

From the very beginning, Christians felt compelled to worship *together*. Because they all equally shared Christ, they could hardly conceive of being apart from one another on the Lord's Day. Early Christians understood the mystery that, as Christ drew near to them in His true body and blood, they were drawn near to one another as His Body on earth. This meant that every aspect of their lives would be shared with one another. The sacramental union in which they participated had practical consequences in how they lived and related to one another.

Portions of our orders of worship are very ancient—especially elements of the Communion liturgy. One writing called the *Didache* (the "Teachings of the Apostles") dates to about AD 140 and includes a beautiful eucharistic prayer:

> **As this piece [of bread] was scattered [as grain] over the hills and then was brought together and made one, so let your Church be brought together from the ends of the earth into your kingdom. For yours is the glory and the power through Jesus Christ forever.**[1]

9. **How does the image of individual grains brought together to form one loaf of bread deepen our understanding of worshiping *together*?**

1 Cyril C. Richardson, ed. and trans., "The Teaching of the Twelve Apostles, Commonly Called the Didache," in *Early Christian Fathers*, vol. 1 of The Library of Christian Classics (Philadelphia: Westminster, 1953), 175.

10. Read Romans 12:3–8; Ephesians 4:1–6; and 1 Corinthians 12:12–27. How might thinking about Christian unity in this way encourage us? Is there anything in it that you find convicting?

Paul's teaching compels us to not think of ourselves in isolation from one another. He doesn't say, "Strive to be the body of Christ," but rather, "You *are* the body of Christ" (1 Corinthians 12:27, emphasis added). Since we *are* one Body, since we have been baptized into *one* communion, and since we are all under *one* Head, who is Christ, should we not also worship regularly together?

The book of Exodus records the dramatic account of the Lord delivering His people from their slavery in Egypt. Their first response after crossing the Red Sea was to worship. Liberated together, they also praised together.

11. Read the first couple of verses of the Israelites' salvation song in Exodus 15:1–2. Do you notice anything particular about the use of pronouns here? How is this similar to Paul's description of being one body?

As God's new covenant people, we sing a salvation song unto Christ, our Passover Lamb. Through Baptism, we together have crossed through death to life and have been liberated from the slavery of sin for all eternity. We join our individual "I will sing" into one unified song of a delivered people.

After delivering His chosen people from Egypt, the Lord revealed to them the Law on Mount Sinai. As such, He also revealed His will for them. Through Moses, the Lord reminded them of all He had done for them and exhorted them to obey Him and keep His covenant.

12. **Read the Israelites' response in Exodus 19:7–8. Why is it significant that "all the people answered together"?**

13. **Both individual and cooperate songs and prayers fill the Psalms. You can find the most intimate, personal expressions of anguish or repentance, as well as the most jubilant expressions of public praise. Read Psalm 95:1–7, a song of public praise still used today and known as the Venite. Now read Psalm 42. This psalm is sung out of loneliness and longing for both God and the community (see v. 4). Can you think of a time in your life when Psalm 95 would have been an appropriate response? What about Psalm 42?**

The Bible does not set individual, personal expressions of piety against cooperate worship; they are not at odds. Indeed, we can find positive examples of both throughout the Scriptures. The tendency among North American Christians today, however, is to become more and more isolated from the fellowship of believers. An overemphasis on an individual, personal relationship with God, coupled with unprecedented advancements in technology, has contributed to plummeting worship attendance. Cooperate worship—a community of faith receiving together God's grace, hearing together His Word, and grafted together as one Body—was the default throughout the Old and New Testaments. Isolation or separation, though permitted and at times salutary, was the exception.

Consider the blessing and benefits of being with the Body of Christ in worship. It encourages us to get outside of ourselves in love and service toward others. It forces us to curb our sometimes self-serving ways. It helps us see ourselves as part of something greater and connects us mysteriously with the church throughout time and space.

The life of our Lord Jesus exemplifies a sanctified balance: while He frequently turned to His heavenly Father in personal prayer and devotion, He never neglected the fellowship of cooperate worship and, indeed, drew strength and encouragement from it.

If I feel like I don't get anything out of liturgical worship, should I find another way to worship?

Lutheran pastor and theologian Dietrich Bonhoeffer wrote concerning singing in Christian worship: "It is the voice of the church that is heard in singing together. It is not I who sing, but the church. However, as a member of the church, I may share in its song."[2]

1. **What do you think he meant by the statement "It is not I who sing, but the church"? When you see yourself in worship, do you picture yourself as an individual or as a larger body of believers? Which aspects of worship are individual? Which are corporate?**

There is perhaps no aspect of the Christian life more important than worship, yet it sometimes seems to be the most controversial topic in Christian circles. How should we worship? What styles are appropriate? How do we even define worship? What does the Bible have to say about worship? Let's explore these questions together while also renewing our fervency for the worship of our God, Father, Son, and Holy Spirit.

2 Dietrich Bonhoeffer, *Life Together: The Classic Exploration of Christian Community*, ed. Geffrey B. Kelly (Minneapolis: Fortress Press, 2005), 68.

2. **The word *worship* comes from an old Anglo-Saxon word, *weorthscipe*, which indicated the worthiness of something ("worth-ship"). At its heart, then, worship acknowledges the worthiness of something outside ourselves. In the Bible, the word *worship* is used to describe the ritual activities of the Old Testament (Romans 9:4), as well as the act of bowing down in adoration before someone (Luke 24:52; Matthew 2:11). How might the etymology of the word *worship* give us a new perspective on our own worship?**

3. **In an inspired twist, Paul redefines a Greek word associated with the carrying out of religious duties (*latreia* = "service" or "worship") and applies it to the whole of the Christian life. Take a close look at Romans 12:1–3. What might it mean to think of your whole self as a spiritual act of worship?**

Worship is not just an activity we do for an hour on Sunday mornings, as important as this might be. As "living sacrifice[s]" (Romans 12:1), we offer ourselves *alive*; we are not burnt or consumed as were the Old Testament offerings. We also offer ourselves "in life"—that is, we offer our lives in love and service to the world.

4. **When you hear the word *liturgical*, what comes to mind?**

In the ancient Greco-Roman world, a *leiturgia* (lay-tur-GEE-ah) was a service performed for the state. In the Bible, it's almost always connected to religious activities, or "services." Thus, Zechariah the priest, the father of John the Baptist, "when his time of service [*leiturgia*] was ended," returned home (Luke 1:23). In a way, any type of religious activity or worship service can be considered "liturgical." The important question is not so much "Is it liturgical?" but rather "What *type* of liturgy is used and where is its focus?"

5. **In your mind, what elements are essential for a worship service? How do you think these should be decided?**

Some Christian denominations focus on the "experience" of worship—what I get out of it and how it makes me feel about my relationship with God. Others emphasize the prayers, rites, and services as a work I'm performing before God—something I'm doing to make things right between us. The Lutheran tradition speaks clearly about worship as the place where we receive God's gifts. That is, God graciously comes to us offering forgiveness, life, and salvation through the central elements of His Word and Sacraments. We receive Christ in worship, which is far more important than how we feel when we leave or what we do when we're there.

6. **How might the idea that in worship we receive God's gracious gifts change our attitude toward it? Is there ever a time when you don't think you need what the Lord offers in worship?**

There are certainly examples of God's people erupting into spontaneous praise in the Bible, such as Exodus 15:19–21; 1 Samuel 2:1–2; and Luke 1:46–55. However, we also find many instances of preplanned, structured, and coordinated worship in the Bible. The elaborate instructions concerning major Old Testament festivals such as Passover, the Day of Atonement, and the Feast of Tabernacles recorded in Numbers 28–29 are prime examples. Moses prepared a litany of warnings to be read responsively between the priests and the people at Mount Ebal (see Deuteronomy 27:15–26).

7. **The liturgical life of the Israelites often was scripted, as evident in the book of Psalms. Psalms written for specific occasions became treasured resources repeated generation after generation. The best of the spontaneous expressions of praise were recorded and reused. What advantages might there be in these written and repeated liturgies?**

8. **Christian worship has been called various names by different denominations over the centuries. Make a list of all the different titles you've heard used for various worship services (Mass, Sunday Service, Evening Prayer, and so on). Try to include as many different denominations and traditions as possible. How does what you call something affect your expectations of what you receive from it?**

Lutherans have settled upon *Divine Service* as the title for our orders of Communion. Derived from the German word *Gottesdienst* ("God's Service"), the term *Divine Service* has a two-layered meaning: God serves us, and we serve God. You can see how nicely the English reflects the double meaning of the German and how both aspects are present in worship. For example, God comes to us in His Holy Supper, Christ's true body and blood given for us. But we also respond in prayer, praise, offering, and thanksgiving.

9. **Take out a hymnal and a pencil. Turn to a setting of the Divine Service and put a downward arrow lightly in the margins next to the portions that seem to reflect God coming to us. Put an upward arrow for our response to God. Which portions were easy to classify? Which were more difficult? How might this back-and-forth rhythm of worship help you appreciate more deeply the Divine Service?**

10. **If you have a copy of *Lutheran Service Book* (the maroon hymnal), open again to a Divine Service setting. On the right-hand side, Scripture references are printed in small italics. These indicate from where in God's Word the liturgy comes. How many Scripture references are in the setting you're looking at? How might this help you reassess the value of "liturgical worship"?**

11. **Although the Bible does not give us a specific revealed order for worship, it does exhort us to orderly worship. Read 1 Corinthians 14:26–33. Some of what we read here is descriptive rather than prescriptive, but the command for structure rather than chaos is normative. What are some of the core truths of Lutheran theology that should be reflected in how we arrange our worship services?**

Those who study the history and theology of worship will no doubt have heard the Latin phrase *lex orandi, lex credendi* (law of praying, law of believing). The words are fancy, but the concept is rather simple. *How* we worship affects *what* we believe. And the reverse also holds true: *what* we believe affects *how* we worship.

A couple of clear examples might be helpful. If we kneel before receiving Communion, this physical act influences how we think about the Lord's Supper: our practice affects our beliefs. But the reverse is also true. For example, because we believe that what Jesus did on the cross is central to our worship and proclamation, we place its symbol in prominent focus in our worship space: our beliefs affect our practice.

12. **In what ways do your congregation's worship space and worship practices influence your core beliefs? That is, how does what you do affect what you believe? On the other hand, are there also ways that your central Christian convictions could be better reflected in your services?**

The Divine Service as we have it has developed over centuries. When Jesus ascended unto heaven, He left us not with a hymnal but with a commission (Matthew 28:18–20). However, the rich and beautiful history of our services and hymnody have effectively and powerfully proclaimed the truth of the Gospel for centuries. Portions of our Communion liturgy, for example, date back to the second century AD. The New Testament canticles such as "Lamb of God" and the Gloria in Excelsis are from the time of Christ. Old Testament songs like "Thank the Lord" or the Sanctus stretch back hundreds of years earlier.

13. How might an awareness of the antiquity of our services bring inspiration to your congregational worship?

....

....

....

....

We too often evaluate a worship service with the simple litmus "What did I get out of it?" focusing on the experience rather than the content. Seeing worship as the place where the gifts of forgiveness, life, and salvation are conveyed to us through Christ's Word and Sacraments directs the focus away from our feelings about worship and onto the objective promise of Christ's presence. So also, our actions of prayer, praise, and thanksgiving become less about how these things make us feel and more about a Spirit-led response to God's graciousness to us.

Lutheran worship reflects our biblical teachings and serves to confess them clearly. Seeing the service as Christ's gift of grace to us, flowing from the cross and the empty tomb, helps refocus our personal preferences for style and music toward the content of the Gospel itself. Mature Christians will be able to have charitable disagreements about these matters while also being willing to reexamine their own biases and presuppositions.

Closing Prayer

I praise You, almighty God, that You call Your people together to receive the gifts of forgiveness, life, and salvation. Grant that we might joyfully respond to these gifts and that all our worship might be in spirit and in truth, through Jesus Christ our Lord. Amen.

SESSION 8

ABOUT THE WORLD

MISCONCEPTIONS ABOUT THE WORLD

- **As we witness to the world, the Scriptures are all we need to know.**
- **Calling non-Christian people to repentance for sin will only offend them; we should just talk to them about God's love.**
- **The church should not take a position on issues such as abortion, gender identity, LGBTQIA+ issues, and the like; that's just politics.**

Opening Prayer

Dear Jesus, You came to seek and to save the lost. Form our hearts to be like Yours, so that just as You rescued us from sin and death, we may share Your grace and truth with the world, causing joy in heaven to resound over even one sinner who repents and is gathered into Your strong and saving arms. Amen.

Introduction

Witnessing, repentance, cultural questions—these are some huge topics that often stir up emotions and deep-seated values. Let's start off this final session with some reassurance from God in His Word about who we are, who He is, and how we can engage with the world.

Please be assured about one fact as you look at a very big world in need of God's help, guidance, and rescue: this is God's world. We care about people and try to manage the chaotic gyrations of history, but the world is not ours.

We govern nations and own real estate, but our ruling and possessing are temporary. We get up in the morning, make decisions, go about our work, attend school, and enjoy friendships and family, but we're here for just a season. This is God's world. All people are His people. Psalm 24:1–2 declares, "The earth is the LORD's and the fullness thereof, the world and those who dwell therein, for He has founded it upon the seas and established it upon the rivers." The Creator of all carries everything and everyone on His shoulders.

There are times when you may think the weight of the world is on *your* shoulders. You want people to be okay. You care about their lives now, and you want them to be blessed in eternity. But as you see the problems and pain in the world around you and as you encounter people with genuine needs, your worry and anxiety levels may become elevated because you start to believe that everything depends on you. You become the "worrier-in-chief" for all humanity—or at least for your family or workplace or community. As you face perplexing cultural questions and seemingly impossible obstacles that stand in the way of faith in God, you may think that the barriers are insurmountable and that the true God has no chance in this world that has gone so astray.

That's why it is so important to get a healthy dose of perspective as you contemplate the complexities of the world. The world isn't yours. There is no job opening on indeed.com for the Lord and Savior of the world. That job is taken by Jesus. Remember what God's Word says about Jesus:

> **He is the image of the invisible God, the firstborn of all creation. For by Him all things were created, in heaven and on earth, visible and invisible, whether thrones or dominions or rulers or authorities—all things were created through Him and for Him. And He is before all things, and in Him all things hold together. (Colossians 1:15–17)**

That includes you, everyone in this world, and the entire universe. Take a deep breath and understand that, as the song says, God's got the whole world in His hands. He can handle everything the world throws His way.

He is also actively pursuing His precious people. Psalm 19:1–4 says,

> **The heavens declare the glory of God, and the sky above proclaims His handiwork. Day to day pours out speech, and night to night reveals knowledge. There is no speech, nor are there words, whose voice is not heard. Their voice goes out through all the earth, and their words to the end of the world.**

Luther noted that this psalm "prophesies that the Gospel will be preached in the whole world. . . . For it appears that Christ's kingdom is weak and that Christendom will run aground and be ruined. But this psalm teaches that Christ and His Gospel cannot be hindered any more than one can hinder the course of the sun" (*Luther's Works*, vol. 12, 139). God is not twiddling His thumbs while the world spins out of control. He is making Himself known. Romans 1:18–20 says,

> **For the wrath of God is revealed from heaven against all ungodliness and unrighteousness of men, who by their unrighteousness suppress the truth. For what can be known about God is plain to them because God has shown it to them. For His invisible attributes, namely, His eternal power and divine nature, have been clearly perceived, ever since the creation of the world, in the things that have been made. So they are without excuse.**

People have consciences, and God is working on those consciences as He makes Himself known. Paul spoke about the people of the world in Romans 2:15: "They show that the work of the law is written on their hearts, while their conscience also bears witness, and their conflicting thoughts accuse or even excuse them." When you wonder if people will ever see their emptiness, sin, and need for something more than this confused, chaotic, and God-rejecting world offers, you can be assured that God is working on them.

But how will people hear and receive the blessing of forgiveness and salvation? How will they meet their Rescuer and Redeemer? That is God's work too. Ephesians 2:5 states clearly that God, "even when we were dead in our trespasses, made us alive together with Christ—by grace you have been saved." The fate of the world is a matter of God's heart. The One who created the world and all who live in it is also the One who took the initiative to save it—and still reaches actively to seek and to save the lost. Romans 5:8 brings Good News: "God shows His love for us in that while we were still sinners, Christ died for us." God's got this.

In a world where possessions, success, health, intellect, relationships, and life itself are temporary, God provides the only lasting solution. Throughout history, people have offered pathways to peace through philosophies, good works, and humanly developed religions. Each one involved some sort of human effort to achieve unity with a higher power or a state of inner contentment. But never in history has any person, movement, or kingdom suggested what the world really needs: a savior. The world needed to be rescued from human powerlessness, decay, and fallenness. That's where the wisdom, truth, and grace of God broke into the same-old, same-old menu of human solutions.

The apostle Peter declared, "There is salvation in no one else, for there is no other name under heaven given among men by which we must be saved" (Acts 4:12). What name was he talking about? Jesus. Yes, Jesus is the only Savior ever revealed in history. And He is what the world needs—His life lived perfectly for us, His death on the cross to carry our sins, His resurrection from the grave to conquer the curse of death, and His promised return to usher in a new creation where God "will wipe away every tear . . . and death shall be no more, neither shall there be mourning, nor crying, nor pain anymore" (Revelation 21:4).

This unique and life-giving message is what you have the privilege of sharing with the world. You get to be part of this blessed mission of salvation. God equips you and uses you to share the way, and the truth, and the life with others. When you share this Good News, you are not imposing a hardship on people's lives or intruding with a heavy-handed message. You're doing people a favor. You're bringing the only lasting source of soul restoration, heart encouragement, and everlasting blessing. You are bringing the gift everyone needs. But you need not carry the burden of the outcome. God is the one who produces the results. Paul said clearly, "I planted, Apollos watered, but God gave the growth. So neither he who plants nor he who waters is anything, but only God who gives the growth" (1 Corinthians 3:6–7).

As you face this big, wild, challenging, and unpredictable world filled with more people and problems than anyone could ever figure out, don't be afraid. Don't lose heart. Don't believe the devil's lie that all is lost. Remember, "God gave us a spirit not of fear but of power and love and self-control" (2 Timothy 1:7). Confidence in God's faithfulness is founded on the resurrection of Jesus. Confidence in His continuing work is located in His means of grace, which work in people's lives and hearts. Through His Word, the gift of Baptism, and the blessing of the Lord's Supper, God delivers the gifts of forgiveness and salvation earned by Jesus through His death and resurrection. As you share God's Word of life, God's promise brings certainty and encouragement:

> **For as the rain and the snow come down from heaven and do not return there but water the earth, making it bring forth and sprout, giving seed to the sower and bread to the eater, so shall My word be that goes out from My mouth; it shall not return to Me empty, but it shall accomplish that which I purpose, and shall succeed in the thing for which I sent it. (Isaiah 55:10–11)**

This is your confidence and your Gospel foundation as you encounter the world. Now, let's tackle some big questions together.

As we witness to others, are the Scriptures all we need to know?

As you face a complicated world filled with complex issues, you can take heart that the Word of God is a living and active instrument of the Holy Spirit (see Hebrews 4:12). It is the powerful sword of the Spirit that foils the devil's destructive work and breaks through his interfering barriers (see Ephesians 6:17). God's Word is your best source for sharing God's hope and salvation with the world. But there are times you may be afraid that you won't know what to say or won't know enough as you talk to people about faith. What if you say the wrong thing or freeze when given the opportunity to share the Gospel? How can you prepare to face the world as a witnessing Christian? Should you start memorizing key Bible passages and central doctrinal truths? What is the best way to begin?

1. **Read Luke 10:1–2 and Ephesians 6:18–20. According to these verses, what is the first component needed as you face a world separated from God?**

Prayer places you in humble dependence on the Lord of the harvest, asking Him to send workers and relying on His Spirit for opportunities to share the mystery of the Gospel. Prayer will vanquish anxiety and safeguard your heart, just as Paul urged in Philippians 4:6–7.

2. **Read 1 Kings 19:14–18. What comfort and encouragement did God give Elijah as he faced a hostile culture and world? How do you see God provide this for you as you face the world?**

You may feel alone and defeated at times, but you can take heart in God's promise, presence, and ongoing help. He will never leave you or forsake you (see Deuteronomy 31:8).

3. **Read Psalm 119:105; Jonah 3:1–10; and Hebrews 4:12. What do these verses teach about the work of God's Word? What confidence do these verses provide as you share His Word with others?**

It's so important to "let the word of Christ dwell in you richly" (Colossians 3:16). Commit a favorite Bible verse to memory so you can share the comfort and blessing it provides. Add favorite verses as you find them. They will provide power and blessing to others as you share the hope you have in Jesus.

4. **Write a favorite Bible verse below. Work on memorizing it so you can share it with others who need God's comfort, encouragement, and truth.**

5. **Read Matthew 28:16–20. How do these verses inform and guide you as you share your faith with others?**

So, how can we share the saving message of Jesus with people in our lives? Let's look at four aspects of the Matthew passage above to guide us.

First, be in relationship with Jesus. The disciples went to Galilee to meet Jesus in the place He instructed. You meet Jesus in His Word. Jesus promised,

> **But the Helper, the Holy Spirit, whom the Father will send in My name, He will teach you all things and bring to your remembrance all that I have said to you. Peace I leave with you; My peace I give to you. Not as the world gives do I give to you. Let not your hearts be troubled, neither let them be afraid. (John 14:26–27)**

This is the Word that provides the content of your message and the power to transform lives. Your key to sharing the Gospel is the Word of God. God's revealed Word brings the Good News of salvation that broke into the world from the outside. Sharing Jesus with others means, first, being immersed in His Word.

Second, be in relationship with others. Jesus gave His disciples the mandate to go and make disciples of all nations. Just as Jesus, the friend of sinners, reached out to the least and lost, He calls you to form relationships with people so you can share His love, His forgiveness, and the gift of eternal life with them. In a world that gravitates toward isolation, where loneliness plagues the culture and where relationships are replaced with cyber interactions and online transactions, God created the church, His people, to reflect His personal and relational reach into people's lives. You earn the trust and credibility to share God's Good News when you invest your time and sincere effort to cultivate genuine relationships with people in your life. There is no need to be afraid that people's sins, choices, lifestyles, or beliefs will be too much for the Word of God. No one is outside of God's reach of grace and truth. Take an interest in people. Listen. Take time. The most meaningful conversations happen when you are truly sharing your life with another person.

Third, use the gifts God provides. Jesus said that disciples are made through Baptism and God's Word.

6. **How can you use God's Word to share the Good News of Jesus with people in your life? Consider ways for each of the categories below.**

- **In prayer:**
- **In writing:**
- **In speaking:**
- **Online:**

Fourth, trust that Jesus is with you as you share. Jesus promised, "I am with you always, to the end of the age" (Matthew 28:20). Jesus is with you as you encounter the challenges of the world. He walks with you as you connect with people. He wants all people to know Him and the life He gives even more than you do. You can be confident that Jesus will use you as an instrument in His hand as you share His love and new life with others.

7. **Read John 4:4–26. As you ponder your encounters with people who may not know Jesus, what do you learn from Jesus' conversation with the woman at the well?**

Sharing your faith doesn't involve a formula or a gimmick. People are gripped by truth. The people in your life are touched and impacted when you are clear about what you know and what you don't know.

What don't you know? You don't know God's timing. You can't comprehend the intricacies of God's plan. You aren't able to fathom the mysteries of tragedy and trial this side of heaven. You can't always answer the question "Why?" or provide the reasons for a seemingly unanswered prayer. You don't know when Jesus will return. God's plans and ways transcend our understanding, as He Himself declared in Isaiah 55. There is a lot you don't know and will never know.

But there is so much you *do* know! You know where God can be found. He speaks through His Word. God works through Baptism. God also gives the gifts of His presence and forgiveness in the Lord's Supper. God is found in Word and Sacrament. You can let people know where to meet Him.

You also know God's plan of salvation. Jesus was sent "to seek and to save the lost" (Luke 19:10). God's plan is a plan of salvation through the life, death, resurrection, ascension, and return of Jesus. God's plan is to bless His precious people with the forgiveness of sins, strength for each day, and the gift of eternal life. God does not want to lose anyone. Jesus said, "And this is the will of Him who sent Me, that I should lose nothing of all that He has given Me, but raise it up on the last day" (John 6:39). Jesus died for all (see 2 Corinthians 5:14). God wants everyone to be saved (see 1 Timothy 2:4). You can share the certainty of God's life-saving plan with people in your life.

Finally, you know that through joy and through struggle, God does not leave or forsake you. At the end of the Gospel of Matthew, Jesus uttered one of the greatest promises anyone could ever receive: "And behold, I am with you always, to the end of the age" (Matthew 28:20). Life might be sailing along without a care, or it may be a journey more difficult than you could ever imagine. Either way, Jesus is present with His grace, strength, comfort, and care. The apostle Paul articulated the powerful promise: "For I am sure that neither death nor life, nor angels nor rulers, nor things present nor things to come, nor powers, nor height nor depth, nor anything else in all creation, will be able to separate us from the love of God in Christ Jesus our Lord" (Romans 8:38–39). You can share that promise of God's presence with everyone.

Be clear about what you know and what you don't know. The devil will try to convince you that you need to be able to explain everything about God's timing and plan before you tell people about Him. Then Satan will tempt you to doubt what you do know: the certain presence of God, His plan of salvation, and the certain places He speaks and gives His gifts. Instead of directing people to the certain words and promises of God, Satan would have you clam up in confusion, become preoccupied with puzzling theological debates, and hesitate to teach, proclaim, and live the clear truths that Jesus provides.

So, what do you do? Admit what you don't know and share what you do know. As you share Christ with others, hold on to Jesus' promise: "Come to Me, all who labor and are heavy laden, and I will give you rest" (Matthew 11:28).

Won't a call to repentance for sin offend people who aren't Christians? Can we just talk to them about God's love?

Sin has never been a popular word. Being confronted with personal faults, failures, and foibles has seldom been a pleasant experience for anyone. No one craves a conversation about their own imperfection. Does that mean a truth-filled conversation about the human condition is an impossibility as you reach out to people who do not have faith in Jesus?

This is where God's Word offers help in effectively communicating the truth of humanity's fall into sin and the need for repentance. God cared about people too much to only offer a surface-level explanation of our hopeless situation. In addition to using the word *sin* to describe what separates us from God, the Bible digs deeply into the nuances of humanity's condition. These facets of fallenness may help communicate the need for repentance and forgiveness in a way that moves people's hearts to see their need for God's help.

"To sin" is one translation of two different Greek words: *hamartano* and *skandalizo*. The words are used forty-three and twenty-nine times, respectively, in the New Testament.

Hamartano points to errors, committing an offense against God or someone else: "If your brother sins against you, go and tell him his fault, between you and him alone. If he listens to you, you have gained your brother" (Matthew 18:15). A helpful question to ask people who may be exploring their spiritual condition could be this: "When you look in the mirror every day, what flaws or mistakes stand out in your life?"

Skandalizo is similar to its English derivative, *scandalize*. It means "to cause an offense": "If your right eye causes you to sin, tear it out and throw it away. For it is better that you lose one of your members than that your whole body be thrown into hell" (Matthew 5:29). This word refers to public wrongdoing as well as hidden impurity. A helpful question as you dialogue with a person about spiritual matters may be to ask, "What secrets are bringing struggle and shame into your life?"

Another word used in the Bible in relation to our sinful condition is *trespass* (in Greek, *paraptoma*). It is used nineteen times in the New Testament and means "an act that goes beyond healthy boundaries": "For if many died through one man's trespass, much more have the grace of God and the free gift by the grace of that one man Jesus Christ abounded for many" (Romans 5:15). The word can point out how we go too far at times: excessive drinking, spending, eating, anger, and more. Consider this a helpful question in a dialogue with people who are open to reflecting on the reality of their lives: "How are you hurting yourself or other people by crossing lines of healthy behavior?"

Romans 3:23 adds another nuance to sin: "For all have sinned [*hamartano*] and fall short [*hystereo*] of the glory of God." *Hystereo* is used sixteen times in the New Testament and means "to lack or fall short." This is a powerful description of what vexes modern lives and highlights our need for God's help (think of the English word *hysteria*). You may lead people to realize their need with this question: "Have you noticed that you're not able to keep up with the fast pace, with housework, with email, with laundry, with work demands? How is running out of time, energy, and resources affecting you?"

"Lawlessness" is yet another description of the broken state of humanity. The Greek word is *anomia*, and it is used fifteen times in the New Testament. Jesus said about the days before His return, "And because lawlessness will be increased, the love of many will grow cold" (Matthew 24:12). Sometimes the word is translated as "wickedness." Start a discussion that may help highlight the fouled-up human condition by asking, "What chaos and coldness of heart do you see increasing in the world these days?"

God's description of sin goes deep and covers the gamut of trouble and chaos we encounter and cause in this world. As you dialogue with people, remember that these biblical descriptors of sin accuse the broken human soul and capture the ache and woundedness of a person's heart. When you talk about sin with people, they may very well need a word that awakens their conscience. Sometimes, however, people will crave truth that reveals and addresses their hurt and struggle. The world tries to deny this persistent pain or seeks to anesthetize the sense that something is missing.

God's Word exposes the real issues and problems. The Scriptures diagnose the brutal truth of being separated from God. The Law shows our sin, making our hearts ready for a solution: repentance and forgiveness.

1. **Read Galatians 5:19–21. What questions might spring from this catalog of human depravity as you dialogue with people about the sinful nature of humanity?**

2. **Read Acts 2:36–41. What does it mean to repent? How is a person brought to repentance?**

We need repentance regularly. Luther noted in the first of his Ninety-Five Theses: "When our Lord and Master Jesus Christ said, 'Repent' (Mt 4:17), he willed the entire life of believers to be one of repentance" (*Luther's Works*, vol. 31, 25). This was the message of Jesus' first sermon: "Repent and believe in the gospel" (Mark 1:15).

The Augsburg Confession states, "Now, strictly speaking, repentance consists of two parts. One part is contrition, that is, terrors striking the conscience through the knowledge of sin. The other part is faith, which is born of the Gospel [Romans 10:17] or the Absolution and believes that for Christ's sake, sins are forgiven. It comforts the conscience and delivers it from terror" (Article XII, paragraphs 3–5).

Repentance turns us around and returns us to our gracious God. The Lutheran Confessions boldly label repentance as "God's thunderbolt":

> **By the Law He strikes down both obvious sinners and false saints. He declares no one to be in the right, but drives them all together to terror and despair. . . . This is not . . . manufactured repentance. It is . . . true**

> **sorrow of heart, suffering, and the sensation of death. This is what true repentance means. (Smalcald Articles, Part III, Article III, paragraphs 2–3)**

The purpose of repentance is not to be swallowed up by guilt. It is to be freed from a dark and destructive direction by God's wakening Word and to be sent on a new path by the sin-conquering Savior. The Lutheran Confessions note,

> **If you live in repentance, you walk in Baptism. For Baptism not only illustrates such a new life, but also produces, begins, and exercises it. For in Baptism are given grace, the Spirit, and power to suppress the old man, so that the new man may come forth and become strong [Romans 6:3–6]. (Large Catechism, Part 4, paragraphs 75–76)**

Repentance is a gift of God. As you dialogue with people about their broken condition, you can also call them back to the open arms of the Savior. By God's grace, through the work of the Holy Spirit, He will grant repentance that leads to new life. Paul assured Timothy that, by correcting his opponents with gentleness, "God may perhaps grant them repentance leading to a knowledge of the truth" (2 Timothy 2:25).

3. **Read John 1:17; Ephesians 2:1–9; and 1 John 1:5–10. How would you define *Law* and *Gospel*? What is the best way to share the Law and Gospel with people who are trapped in their sin?**

....

....

....

....

....

....

All conversations with people in the world revolve around Law and Gospel. Either sin is being exposed and acknowledged, or guilt and shame are being alleviated with the promise and assurance of God's forgiveness through Jesus Christ.

Applying these two messages requires attentive listening, fervent prayer, and Spirit-filled discernment. When people are resistant and filled with pride, they most likely need the message of the Law to break through their hardened attitude. When people are struggling, worried, and filled with guilt, they often need to hear the Gospel, the Good News of Jesus Christ, who carries their burden, washes away their sin, and gives them the blessing of eternal hope.

Christians who encounter the world must take sin seriously. If sin isn't addressed with all gravity, Jesus can't be taken seriously. No one needs a Savior if sin is not a problem. The doctrine of sin is a central part of God's revelation. It is a foundational wake-up call for all people. The Bible says, "No one does good, not even one" (Romans 3:12); "all have sinned and fall short of the glory of God" (Romans 3:23); "[we] were by nature children of wrath. . . . We were dead in our trespasses" (Ephesians 2:3, 5); "the whole creation has been groaning" in the brokenness of sin (Romans 8:22). Only with a full understanding of sin does the Good News of God's rescue and relief shine brightly. Speaking the truth about our fallen condition opens people's hearts to their need for the Savior.

Can the church take strong positions on abortion, gender identity, LGBTQIA+ issues, and the like, or is that just politics?

You may have heard this common advice: "Don't talk about religion or politics." Hot topics can be off limits with neighbors, friends, coworkers—and even family. Sometimes followers of Jesus are even scolded for discussing and taking positions on moral and cultural issues. What can you do in a world where issues are becoming more polarizing and divisive than ever?

First, let the Word of God be your guide. Christians are called to speak where God's Word speaks but to be silent where God's Word is silent. If the Scriptures address an issue, it is important for God's people to address it too. The Bible discusses many current issues because they are problems humans have faced throughout history. Topics like marriage, identity, sexuality, and the value of human life appear already in opening chapters of the Bible. Caution always needs to be exercised, however. God's people can never put words in His mouth about issues not addressed in His Word.

Second, remember the main thing. It may be tempting to make a popular media debate the central focus of your faith. But getting caught up in the emotions of cultural and political issues can distract you from God's primary purpose of revealing Himself: to save fallen humanity from sin through the atoning sacrifice of Jesus. The Gospel in a nutshell is John 3:16, but verse 17 reveals God's heart for the world: "For God did not send His Son into the world to condemn the world, but in order that the world might be saved through Him." The main focus as a follower of Jesus is not to concentrate your attention on the latest issues—even very serious ones—but to join Paul in saying, "For I decided to know nothing among you except Jesus Christ and Him crucified." (1 Corinthians 2:2). This is the one thing needed by all people.

Third, beware of getting caught up in arguments. The world wants to pull you into a vocal, vigorous, and sometimes not-so-kind debate about issues. The narrative of the world thrives on division, disagreement, and dislike. The world gravitates toward bad news, hopelessness, sensationalism, comparison, and criticism. Paul offers good counsel about the course God's people need to take.

1. **Read 2 Timothy 2:23–26. How can this guide us when we consider and take positions on cultural issues?**

A Christian can take a strong position about issues, but addressing issues in a Christlike manner may change the minds and hearts of people entrenched in practices and lifestyles that bring pain and hurt to themselves and others.

2. **Read Ephesians 6:10–18. What do these verses say about taking strong positions on issues based in God's Word and the manner in which those issues are addressed with others?**

3. **Read Luke 10:38–42. How are Jesus' words to Martha relevant to engaging with issues of the day?**

4. **Read Colossians 1:9–18. How does each verse shape your approach to encountering the people of the world with the Good News of Jesus?**

Jesus described His redeemed people as the light of the world and as a city set on a hill:

> **You are the light of the world. A city set on a hill cannot be hidden. Nor do people light a lamp and put it under a basket, but on a stand, and it gives light to all in the house. In the same way, let your light shine before others, so that they may see your good works and give glory to your Father who is in heaven. (Matthew 5:14–16)**

This imagery sets the tone for a Christian's approach to the world. God's people are not negative "wet blankets" who take the fun and freedom out of life. People redeemed by Jesus are shining lights in a world of chaos and confusion. They are beacons of spiritual clarity and eternal hope for a world groping in the darkness. Jesus brings the freedom of life in its fullness (see John 10:10) as beloved children of God (see 1 John 3:1). Facing the world means bringing these gifts with confidence and joy.

Closing Prayer

Gracious Lord of all things and Head of the church, grant us wisdom and courage for the facing of this hour. Use us to share Your love and the life You give in Jesus with the world. In Jesus' name. Amen.